a Brief GUIDE

"The first step in controlling the world, is in knowing it."

a Brief GUIDE

to
Understand Everything

by Max Mische

A Brief Guide Publishing

This publication is designed to provide information in regard to a holistic perspective which has the potential to increase ones knowledge.
It is sold with the understanding that the publisher is not engaged in rendering, any business, self-help, or other professional services. If business advice or other expert assistance is required, the services of a competent professional should be sought. All statements of fact are to the best of our knowledge true, but should be verified by specialist documents or persons.

Published by:
A Brief Guide Publishing
Post Office Box 25091
Los Angeles, CA 90025
Orders@understandeverything.com
http://www.understandeverything.com

ISBN   0-9776082-0-4

Library of Congress Cataloguing-in-Publication Data

A Brief Guide to Understand Everything / by Max Mische – 1st ed.

Printed in U.S.A.

Dedicated to the destruction of inequality.

Contents

Introduction

0   **A View to Everything...**
A Perspective on everything
Understanding Everything
Reading this book

1   **The Mind & Self... the foundation to all ones knowledge.**
Know thyself
The Self as Knower
The Self as Known
Perception
Putting it all together

2   **Divisions and Classifications... the breaking up of the whole.**
Evolutionarily created
Effects of Divisions and Classifications
Putting it all together

3   **The System... and the many within.**
Micro-systems
Macro-systems
Putting it all together

4   **Extremes/Opposites... the ends of the spectrum.**
Dualities everywhere
Polar extremes interact
Putting it all together

5   **Cycles... Constant flux among poles**
Regular & Irregular
Extremes Swing to extremes
Putting it all together

6   **Who, What, Why, Where, How... for discovering the truth.**
Skepticism... the art of questioning humanity

Questioning the Natural World
Putting it all together

7   **The Parts become the Whole... constant application**
All the Same; All Different
All or Nothing
Balance
Z, Omega, Death, Fin, End

Appendix

Introduction

A Brief Guide™ to Understand Everything arose after years of study of multiple disciplines. Initially, I was driven to learn about religion, psychology, economics, strategy, politics, biology, and the like as individual subjects for my own personal growth and development. I knew that the more knowledge I acquired, the more I would be able to understand and therefore achieve success in this world.

After a few years of studying, I began to feel as if I was reading the same book, or story, over and over again with only the names of the characters and places differing. Each subject followed similar formulas and patterns that provided a general understanding of each area almost before I even started reading a new book. They all seemed to follow an overall system of laws that dictated each area's existence and survival. They no longer seemed like individual disciplines but instead an overall one.

This is not to say that I could ascertain the specific names of the various principles or things involved with each discipline. However, I could understand the concepts which drove each area. The immense amount of jargon or human coined terminology creates a large roadblock for anyone learning a discipline. Ultimately, all of these names are nothing more than representations of concepts that share similarities.

The basis for the perspective presented in this book was established by my psychological background including my personal study of the world's major religious texts. Most religions present ways of living that are aimed at attaining the good life. Also, most present holistic views of the world in order to provide explanations for its different aspects. As a result of these studies, this book has strong psychological and religious undertones. In many regards, the religious tone in some parts has practical purposes so as to convey the interconnectedness of all things in a simplified manner necessary to distill the world into its basic components.

Some readers will find problems with the book due to this reason. Scientists and researchers in particular will probably take issue with the book's lack of depth due to its holistic approach. Such complaints are reasonable since many of the examples presented could be expanded upon. However, the purpose of this book is to focus on the main principles that will provide a framework that enables one to understand everything without the details. This book draws strongly upon the ancient Taoist text, the "Tao Te Ching," in which Lao Tzu presents a view of the world in 81 brief segments that can be read in less than an hour with no scientific evidence. Such brevity is absolutely necessary in order to allow the mind to use the principles included therein. Periphery things distract from the main point and have been excluded for the most part.

The ancient Taoist tradition has in recent years found a scientific counterpart in Chaos theory. The similarity between the two perspectives is indeed interesting and yields scientific evidence for the ancient tradition of Taoism. The idea of the world having a certain "Way" or being is now represented in equations and formulas in Chaos theory.
However, such correlations are not discussed in depth in this book because of their unnecessary complexity in relation to the main principles discussed here. Let me say again, the purpose of this book is to provide a framework through which everything can be understood.

This book has been marketed for business because business and money in many instances have the most direct practical influence upon an individual's life. An overall understanding of the world enables one to predict and control it thus improving one's life.

Further reading and study of all subject matters is encouraged in order to sharpen the principles contained in this book. One's path to enlightenment never ends, as one's level of understanding of the world can always improve.

Do I contradict myself,
Then I contradict myself,
I am large and contain multitudes
- Walt Whitman

0.

A View to Everything...

Understanding is a
perspective,
not knowledge...

"A Way is a Guide, not a fixed path"

- Lao Tzu

We are all deities, in that we all have untold powers, even though very few ever become actualized. We are deities not in any religious sense, but rather because we have the ability to understand the world and to grow in power from that understanding. In the religious sense, a deity is often omnipotent or nearly so, but as human beings our powers are limited by our bodies, minds, and creations.

At any moment, it is believed the human brain is capable of focusing its attention on only one thing as will be explained later. The ability to understand everything, therefore, requires simplistic principles that the mind can utilize to maximize its capability of understanding.

Because we are looking at basic principles, in-depth knowledge is not a prerequisite to understanding everything. In fact, in-depth knowledge can sometimes hinder one's ability to understand everything, because knowledge can indirectly discourage one from looking at things differently, as one may believe they already understand something. The reality is more likely that he only has a small portion of knowledge. That being said, knowledge is almost always a desirable asset, for the more knowledge one has, the better one is able to think, as one is drawing from a wider range of perspectives and experiences.

Since this book has such a large scope and a short length, it is necessary to introduce the principles of understanding everything, by first using them. The following brief first person narrative employs the principles that are addressed in this book by following a person down a street in London. In many ways, this street could be in any city. The foundation of understanding everything lies in the principles of the mind, divisions and classifications, systems, duality, and cycles.

A Perspective on Everything

As I walk down a residential side road towards Main Street, my awareness of the noise emitting from the upcoming street increases, as though I were approaching a great artery within a body. The corpuscles flow along the street in the form of people walking back and forth—each with a place to go, each with his or her own role to fulfill within the overall system.

As I turn onto Main Street, gas molecules, ever compressing and expanding, impinge on my ears like a symphony of noise, though they are invisible to my eyes. The street is littered with cars and the sidewalks with people. The individuals in the cars seem mysteriously similar to the cars they drive—each possessing internal organs, a means of locomotion, and a need for fuel in order to operate. The sky is overcast, and a nip can be felt in the air due to internal body heat dissipating into the colder environment as the atoms within the body excite the atoms in the air. The people echo the weather, their bodies contracted toward their heated innards with fewer smiles present than can be found in sunnier cities.

Many young women have a focused attention either on the sidewalk or directly ahead of them. This focused attention could be due to a variety of reasons such as from experience that eye contact might be perceived to mean sexual receptivity to a passing male, a result of centuries of oppression from cultural practices, or due to something internal such as the female sexual

14

hormone of estrogen.

A correlation seems to exist between the speed with which a woman walks and her beauty as the most beautiful walk the fastest, possibly indicating a value placed upon beauty as a result of years of evolution selecting for the healthiest, most adapted, individuals. Additionally, cards inside some phone booth walls have pictures of nude women with phone numbers and come-ons such as "For a Good Time," while corresponding cards of males are not present.

Contrariwise, a larger portion of males look at the females, driven by different motivations and internal mechanisms. As opposed to the more contained movements of the females, the males tend to be more outwardly directed in their walks, as if displaying power for others to view—like a peacock showing his feathers or a pigeon on the sidewalk bobbing his head and cooing, conveying power and sexual prowess and thereby instinctively attracting the females, who seek mates capable of producing and in the case of human beings, raising successful children.

Passing a couple, the male holds his female partner close to his side, protecting, showing his care for her, and at the same time staking out his claim upon her. Looking into their minds through knowledge of the ephemeral nature of all things, one sees the doubt, however small, surrounding the strength of their relationship, owing to their combined anxieties, particularly solitude and death. With a world that is ever shrinking in size through improved transportation, the availability and quantity of potential mates is increasing. This increase undoubtedly has a negative impact upon the strength of relationships.

The buildings that line the street are all made of brick, which indicates several things. The island of Britain must not lie on any fault lines—for if it did, the buildings are not likely to have stood for centuries, as bricks are likely to crack and would be inelastic in the event of an earthquake. Likewise, it appears that this is an island not created from volcanic activity like the Hawaiian Islands were, but rather one that had become disconnected from its former continent as a result of rising oceans and shifts of the tectonic plates.

A mailbox painted red has the words "Royal Mail" written across the area above the drop slot. The color red has often been associated with royalty; and even more obviously, the words "Royal Mail" would indicate (if it was not known already) that this country is or once was based upon a monarchical system.

A beggar on the side of the street sits strategically next to an ATM machine repeating a mantra of words: "Spare any change? Cheers. Thanks, sir," over and over again, as he lowers his head thereby yielding power to each passing pedestrian. A man in a business suit walks by, seemingly two inches taller than everyone else; he lets his suit inflate his mind as to who he actually is, though in reality he is naked and fragile, just like the beggar. A Mercedes-Benz passes an older Ford Orion on the road. The majority of cars are of average value, with some on both ends of the price spectrum. This area's class system, then, reveals itself as somewhat mixed though tending towards the lower end.

Many signs are displayed in windows with the words "Internet here" or "Internet Café," indicating a technologically developed nation wherein ordinary people are able to have access to such higher technology. However, it could instead reveal that it is not as developed as other places in which Internet cafés are *not* to be found, due to most people having Internet capability in their own homes. Or perhaps it merely indicates a community filled with transient travelers. The numerous "international calling shops" are possible evidence for this assumption

The streets are, indeed, filled with an international mix of people. Many of them are wearing clothing of their native lands, which indicates with a certain level of probability that they are recent immigrants to the country. Few people from the Orient are visible, possibly indicating that this land is far removed or relatively inaccessible from that part of the world. However, many Africans, Caribbeans, and other Europeans are visible. On the whole, the area seems to be basically lower to middle-class, which is typical for many multicultural areas where new immigrants are trying to make it in a new land.

16

Looking at the heads of everyone walking by, one imagines all of the thoughts and sensations running through their minds. The electricity can almost be felt as neurons fire in their brains while they take in all of the different stimuli, their actions revealing their insides. The DNA within their cells is, like their past experiences, expressed by their exteriors with each wrinkle and curve a product. In the future, full body scans and software to decipher the scans may yield a digital copy of the genetic coding of the person. But until such technologically advanced times, each person is completely unaware of what everyone is thinking and experiencing. Everyone is alone in their own minds looking for others in which to relate to in order to establish connections outside of their minds.

A large number of pubs are prevalent along with some drunken older males, indicating moderate levels of cell death in the brains that pass by. Alcohol and drug use provides another, albeit mostly harmful, means that people can use to temporarily escape from their own thoughts or just to make social connections easier, thereby grounding people in the present rather than the past or future.

The light beam shining through a clearing in the clouds warms my face. This light, as we are told by scientists, exists as a duality, having properties of both particles and waves. The energy from the light warms my face by exciting my skin's atoms. The chlorophyll in the plants along the street solidifies this light energy into glucose for the plants' own fuel needs, in the process releasing oxygen and producing food for the animals of the planet.

One can almost picture the Earth among the other planets in the solar system, traveling around the Sun. The continent of Europe now has its face directed to the Sun, which provides energy in the form of heat and food to sustain the many cycles existing on this planet, such as the hydrological, reproductive, and energy cycles to name only a few.

The carbon atoms bonded in various molecular chains, with fourteen electrons in seven separate orbits, all become increasingly energized due to the energy from the sun. The colors in the area lit by it become more vibrant as the cones in peoples' eyes are better able to receive information on account of the increased light, while the rods, which perceive lightness, become saturated.

As I think, I feel a pressurized sensation due to the use of my brain, as more blood flows to the brain due to increased energy needs from the fast firing neurons. It's a distinctly different feeling than the one a person gets from training his muscles, though both are due to increased blood flow to each area due to increased energy needs from increased usage.

The trees scattered along several side streets are barren, so it must be either winter or the beginning of spring. The sidewalk is littered with cigarette butts and pieces of chewing gum. Freud might suggest that all of these remnants are due to humans' inherent oral fixation, which all mammals have since birth. This oral fixation is spawned from the "suckling reflex" that infants have in order to acquire milk from their mothers. The use of the mouth is a source of comfort throughout the lifetime of a mammal—or, alternatively, a means of relieving stress and distracting the mind.

Large red double-decker buses pass by, showing off part of the city's transportation system, which also includes a rather intricate subway system. The buses appear to be in good condition and relatively new, indicating a wealthy society that can afford to pay for such luxuries as a good transportation system that can be cheap enough to be used by the lower classes.

Cars stopped at a light lurch forward when the light turns green, the tires being the first parts of the car to move while the body, possessing inertia, tries to remain at rest. Everything is constantly being pushed toward the ground because of the Earth's gravitational pull, created by the high velocity of the planet's rotational spin, which also gives us night and day.

A bridge for trains is overhead, with the label "Metropolitan 1914" on its side. Knowing European history allows one to draw the conclusion that this bridge, along with this extension to the rail system, was built during the buildup leading to World War I, in order to have a better system of transportation so that troops and supplies could be hustled to the frontlines in France as fast as possible.

An air molecule is expired from the lungs of a vagrant who sits on the side of the street with his hat down as he asks for change. This molecule is breathed into the lungs of the passing businessman as he walks by, his neurons firing at an accelerated rate owing to the contents of the now empty Starbucks™ coffee cup that he throws into the nearest trash can. The cup will soon begin a journey to its eventual resting place at the nearest landfill, where it will remain for many years while it is transformed by various forces into something else, and recycled back into the Earth.

On a side street, a vein from the main artery, is a stand of fruits and vegetables that have traveled, much like the people, from many environments in other countries. One grew on a tree, another on a vine, another in the ground, but all started from a seed—a bulb—and some indeed are bulbs themselves. Imagine the diversity of genes contained therein, which stay isolated from each other for many years due to uncrossable oceans, each developing their own unique niche within the ecological system.

A German shepherd/Labrador mix sits obediently, unleashed outside of the store its Alpha leader went into. It is a product of several centuries of independent breeding in Germany and the UK, respectively. Several centuries before that, it was the result of the domestication of wild wolves. Selective breeding has brought out the characteristics it now has. It no longer needs to hunt, but instead begs for its food. It is no longer part of a pack of dogs but rather travels with a pack of human beings, with their own distinct hierarchical structure. Its style of play has changed: Instead of "play biting", which once helped it develop survival skills, it now chases Frisbees and tennis balls.

All Europeans and nearly everyone else have encountered each other in times of war. Now, in a world that exists at a general level of peace, the nations' peoples interact freely with one another. Germans walk by Frenchmen. Indians pass by with the same class status as the English.

The clothes everyone wears are in most instances

purposely selected to make a certain statement to the world around them about who the wearer is as a person. Clothes might act to make the wearer more beautiful or different or similar. Then again, clothes might simply be functional to some providing them a means to keep warm.

The dog wears its fur coat, the one that it's had since birth. Despite the seemingly superficial differences, the dog is ultimately no different than the businessman in being a biological entity with all of the cycles that includes. The afflictions that strike some human beings more than others are afflictions based upon basic human weaknesses and chance.

We are even no different than non-biological entities in many ways. The clouds above have the same pattern as do the waves in the sea. In the end, we are all atoms. The carbon atoms partly composing my organs, muscles, bones, and other body parts are no different than the carbon atoms in the soil, in the paper coffee cup, in the bird droppings on the street, or in the pages of this book.

Understanding Everything

Understanding Everything is about grasping the big picture, not the nuts and bolts; the basics, not the details. Society today focuses largely on specialization. As a result, the world is full of experts in very narrow or esoteric fields. A lot of experts, who "learn" verbatim what their books or teachers preach, are a lot like cogs in a machine, performing one task over and over again making small improvements but missing the overall picture.

The person who understands everything is a person who possesses a *perspective* first and knowledge second. He is the one who does not become static, because he is constantly learning. Such a person does not label himself because a label is not necessary and could never describe who he is. Knowledge is helpful in understanding everything, but knowledge is also mostly static.

To understand everything, then, is not to have knowledge

of everything, but rather to have a mind-frame that has the *capability* to understand everything. Now, "everything" does not necessarily imply the specifics. People often get so bogged down analyzing something that they lose sight of the larger picture. There is too much to learn to allow oneself to get bogged down in the details.

This is not to say that you will not understand many complex subjects, for this is not the case. The problem exists when one becomes fixed upon one area of knowledge, biasing one's perspective of how the world actually works.

The basic principles described in this book exist as constructs within our minds—as representations of patterns and characteristics of the world around us. These basic principles apply to everything: from atoms and emotions to the universe in general. Basic principles allow you to understand one entity through knowledge of another, even if the two seem very different. Because of the similarities that exist between elements in our world, the creation of new knowledge, through application of these basic principles, becomes possible once a certain perspective—a new consciousness—has taken hold.

Understanding the basics is a lot like being a ball gently rolling down a hill. As the basics are learned, the ball ever so slightly increases its speed—then increases greatly as one's ability to understand grows, allowing more and more information and knowledge to interact. The only limitation to the ball's speed is the grade of the hill. The only limitation to a person's understanding is their mind.

Reading This Book

To get the most out of this book—and out of anything in general, for that matter—one must concentrate one's mind solely on the purpose of reading the book. That may sound like common sense, but that is why one must pay attention to it, for common sense is commonly disregarded. One who feels that he or she already knows common sense is often the one who does not use it.

Additionally, the mere act of concentration on the single purpose of reading this book will be a form of meditation that neutralizes emotional extremes. Even happiness in excess can be detrimental, for one's mind at such times utilizes rapid assessment techniques, for example in the form of biases, that lead one not to see the absolute truth behind what is actually occurring.

It is imperative to understand that you must not accept anything contained in this book—or anywhere else, for that matter—as fact. Very few things exist in the perceived worlds of our minds that are strictly facts; every piece of information is colored by our own personal perceptions and biases. As Einstein might say, "Everything is relative." *Understanding* means the ability to synthesize the information one already possesses. A flexible understanding is best, allowing for the ability to adapt, and to make use of information. Pieces of knowledge are much like multi-faceted spheres where each facet is another instance of that piece of knowledge. All of the facets together complete the conception of the knowledge. However, at different times, the importance of the number of and the unique facets chosen vary in accordance with the instance at hand. Having the right cognitive tools allows one to make efficient use of knowledge by understanding what is relevant in each particular case.

Because of the immense complexity of each instance of knowledge, independent thought is vital in making the knowledge useful. Knowledge also has an inherent flaw: It is an entity existing within the human mind. In addition, knowledge is fixed, while thought is infinite. However, thought exists only because of knowledge, and vice versa.

In this book, there are eight separate chapters, arranged in such a manner that each builds upon the last one. These divisions in the form of chapters are unfortunate—because each is really part of all the others—but necessary. Being granted but a modest brain in order to perceive the world, humans must gather pieces of information so that they can combine into larger units.

Through the use of the basic principles presented in the

following chapters and by exercising an open and inquisitive mind, the ability to understand everything can be attained. An ancient Japanese Samurai piece of wisdom holds:

The ignorant when told one thing,
understands one thing.
The adept when told one thing,
understands ten.

I.

The Mind & Self...
the foundation to all knowledge

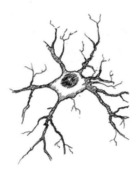

"...to know oneself is the foundation stone of knowledge."

- Douglas MacArthur

The MIND is the most valuable asset that any person could ever possess, and at the same time is something *everyone* possesses. It is the tool that gives rise to your personality, knowledge, thoughts, consciousness, feelings, and reality—and your very existence. The mind is where all of one's knowledge is perceived, interpreted, and stored. It is the basis of knowledge—for knowledge does not exist without a mind for it to exist within. There exists no knowledge in the world itself, for the world does not try to understand itself. Only the minds of animals—in particular, humans—do that.

One of the greatest misfortunes in this life is that upon exiting the mother's womb, one is not given an instruction manual on how to operate this invaluable tool—a tool that alters not only oneself but also the very world in which we live. When you read an instruction manual for any kind of gadget, you are reading for the purpose of utilizing the gadget to its utmost degree. When the "gadget" is your own brain, such utilization is essential, for that is where all information streams into the mind.

25

Intimate knowledge of anything yields the best possible use of whatever one has knowledge of. For where would the racecar driver be if suddenly placed into an unknown vehicle? The painter who switches from acrylics to watercolors? The computer user who switches from a PC to an Apple™? How much more important is this need for intimate knowledge when what needs to be intimately known is the knowledge of oneself?

Additionally, psychological knowledge is exceptionally important in dealing with the ever-increasing dominance of social organizations, imposed upon this world by others with brains in essence no different than yours. While your brain is trying to understand, other brains are trying to deceive. The acquisition of knowledge, therefore, is much like a war, complete with attacks, the search for enclaves of the truth, and defenses which one uses to fight against others who try to compromise one's mind with lies or biases.

Therefore, just as builders begin the process of building a house by laying the foundation, this book begins with the foundation from which all things enter into one's reality. Although this chapter conveys but a small slice of information about the brain, it is nonetheless a brief summary of the key elements that are necessary in order to begin to understand everything.

Know Thyself

"Know Thyself."

The above quotation—on its own, on a pedestal—deserves the greatest consideration of any piece of advice one will ever come across. Any self-help book or any successful individual will almost always cite "Know thyself" as key advice towards success.

The repetition of this quote is by no means a coincidence. For when one views the world, one is viewing oneself. Nothing that one is consciously or unconsciously aware of escapes the filtration process of one's own perception, knowledge, and experiences—and, therefore, of one's biases.

Yet, despite the extreme importance of this maxim, a very small portion of the world's population truly knows itself, and no one ever entirely knows oneself. Ignorance, emotion, and denial abound in peoples' minds, filtering the truth as it enters the mind so as to protect their illusions regarding themselves and the world. Be on guard against those who are deeply infected, for their tainted "knowledge" is not truth, only a distorted view of the truth.

But what is the Self? This is certainly no easy question, but rather extremely complex and somewhat relative, as the Self can be seen from many different perspectives. It is also a question that has been at the heart of many heated debates and much tension and violence throughout human history—largely because of its religious implications, whose discussion will be avoided here.

Instead, our discussion will be loosely structured around the explanation of the Self detailed in *The Principles of Psychology*, by the late nineteenth-century psychologist William James. In James' understanding, the Self is divided into two major components: the Self as knower and the Self as known. The Self as knower is one's consciousness. The Self as known is the part of an individual's self that comprises all of the physical aspects of one's Self, including body, social relations, and property. Despite this distinction, however, these two aspects are intimately connected to each other—and so the following subheadings are only a loose framework.

The Self as Knower (Mind)

The mind is an intangible entity found within the physical human brain. Therefore, in order to discuss the mind, we must first briefly learn a little bit about the structure that encloses it and from which it is spawned.

On the most fundamental known level, our brains are composed of nothing more than atoms, which are in turn made up of electrons, protons, and neutrons. As physicists are discovering, these components in turn, can be broken into even smaller components. In this book, we will discuss only the atoms in the brain, all of which form the molecules constituting the brain cells which enable us to have thoughts, feelings, and consciousness, and indeed, our existence. The pieces of paper that make up this book are, at this fundamental level, no different than you, the reader. Both are constructed out of carbon atoms that bond with various other elements. It is important to understand this similarity, for in order to understand everything, it is necessary to look past the immediate reality in order to see relationships at deeper levels. Everything is the same; everything is different.

We have two types of brain cells, known as neurons and glia. Glia cells are about 50 times more prevalent in the brain than neurons and provide support and nutrition to it. Additionally, they aid in signal transmission for the nervous system, create myelin (the protective sheaths around neurons that insulate sections of them), and maintain homeostasis. One way neurons transmit information is through the use of various neurotransmitters, which travel across the gaps, known as synapses, between cells. The neurotransmitters then induce an electrochemical reaction within the receiving cell, sending forth a burst of electricity that travels down the neuron and initiates the whole cycle again for the next neuron. The totality of all of these signals is what gives one *consciousness*—the ability to think, feel, experience, and be.

Understanding that the Self is comprised of these minute physical interactions is an often overlooked, yet important aspect of one's knowledge of oneself, for we exist as the sum total of all of these interactions. In the bloodstream there is another type of chemical messenger that, like neurotransmitters, helps to pass information to other parts of the body. These messengers are known as hormones. Like neurotransmitters, hormones are constantly undergoing a process of flux inside one's body, playing significant roles in altering the way one perceives, thinks, and behaves.

Realizing that these hormones, particularly the sexual hormones, have a certain pattern of release is important to being

28

able to understand the intricacies of one's patterns of perception that affect everything one experiences and thinks. Most females undoubtedly have a much better understanding of the effects of hormones than males due to their ovulatory cycle which typically lasts for 28 days. During this cycle, hormone levels fluctuate tremendously with the menstrual cycle, which lasts from three to seven days, causing the greatest influx of hormones—in particular, estrogen—into the bloodstream of the female, causing varied alterations in their bodies, mood, thoughts, and behavior.

Males, on the other hand, lack any momentous event, like the riddance of the uterine wall in females during their menstrual cycle. But males have hormonal cycles as well—multiple cycles, in fact, but two main ones. First, testosterone levels vary throughout the day. For most males, testosterone levels peak at around 3 o'clock in the morning, gradually subsiding in the course of the day. The whole cycle starts over the next day.

Testosterone also has a yearly cycle, which is affected by light exposure. Over the yearly cycle, an increase in overall light results in an overall increase in testosterone, and vice versa. This fact can be seen more easily in other animals with fixed reproduction cycles, like reptiles.

For example, all reptile breeders know that in order to induce mating, a period of reduced light and low temperature is necessary before the light and heat are restored to their regular schedule. For when the light returns, a surge of testosterone is released in the males, giving them a desire to mate. This mechanism has played a beneficial role in nature controlling mating so that the initiation of the gestation period is during a time when food is plentiful and the temperature is warm, so as to ensure the proper development of the fetus inside the mother. Today, for many humans, this adaptation is no longer a necessary one—but it still is at work.

Every human being at one point existed as a fetus that exhibited no outward display of either gender. In fact, the default sex is female, for without the presence of testosterone, the non-differentiated genitalia of the fetus will never close into the male genitalia, even if the male sex chromosome is present. Remnants of this early stage are visible on both male and female genitalia, revealing our once undifferentiated state.

Food, in addition to hormones, alters ones brain's chemistry, for it fuels our existence by providing nutrients for our bodies' and brains' growth, maintenance, and energy creation. This alteration can be seen more easily with certain foods than with others, for some foods are responsible for larger fluctuations. For example, several studies have shown that food products derived from soy increase the levels of estrogen in both males and females.

Conversely, up to four drinks of alcohol increases testosterone levels. When linked with testosterone's notoriety for inducing aggressive behavior, such a finding does a lot to explain why over 50 percent of all murders and violent crimes have been committed by individuals under the influence of alcohol.

One of the most influential neurotransmitters, dopamine, is part of what psychologists call the "reward system." For when one engages in an activity that promotes the survival of the organism and the species, dopamine is released in several sections of the brain to reinforce that behavior.

For instance, imagine that you are sitting down eating your favorite food. Your mood rises as a sense of satisfaction enters your mind. This elevation of mood, however, is not due to the food itself, but is rather a result of neurotransmitters in your mind. Partly, the mere act of concentrating on something as mindless as eating has a beneficial effect, but in addition, the brain releases dopamine into the channels between neurons, causing cells to fire and making you feel rewarded because you are providing materials for your body that will allow it to sustain itself.

Dopamine is an evolutionarily created chemical that influences the human being to act so as to ensure its own survival as well as that of the species. For if one were not intrinsically rewarded for carrying on the processes necessary for the survival of your own organism and of the species, what motivation would there be to eat, mate, or, for that matter, live? Dopamine within the brain, therefore, exists to ensure an intrinsic desire for all of the basic survival activities.

Likewise, suppose you have not seen a loved one for a long period of time. The first moment that you see the loved one again, you feel "overcome" by joy. Perhaps no more perfect word could be used, for in a way one really is "overcome" by the natural processes occurring in one's mind. The surge of dopamine unconsciously released by your mind at the initial sight of a loved one is almost impossible to control. The strength of the surge varies in accordance with how close you are to the individual or how long he or she has been away. This surge is due to the innate human need for social relations as they provide a sense of security and comfort. Social relations also help our species through advancements created through cooperative work as well as at a base level to help us pass on our genetic information.

Another function of dopamine is to facilitate learning. For example, imagine you are learning how to perform a new skill—say, rollerblading. At first it is really difficult to even stand on the skates, but once you are able to maintain your balance standing up, you feel like you've accomplished something, and that makes you feel good. What has just occurred, at a neurological level, is that the dopamine cells in the hippocampus (the region attributed to learning) and the somatosensory region (the area responsible for one's sense of body and touch) have just released dopamine into their respective synapses, thus strengthening the neural pathways which just helped you accomplish this feat. Next time, the same activity will be easier to accomplish.

Once the pathways in the brain are well established, however, the reward system ceases to become activated across that particular channel, because its purpose has ceased to exist. You have learned the skill, and the connection has been made. The feeling of accomplishment disappears; reinforcement is no longer necessary.

The dopamine reinforcement pattern, as well as other neurotransmitter-based systems, can be stimulated "artificially" as well, through drugs. Being able to artificially induce the same

31

effect as entities that promote the survival of the species—or a much greater one—can be very dangerous, however, for it can induce dependency on harmful substances used to achieve a "high" feeling. Dependency causes the brain to adapt to the drug, causing the "high" to be "lower" after each use, as the drug over saturates the system. The much higher "high" attained through artificial means, may cause one to lose interest in things naturally enjoyable and beneficial.

Do not think, however, that "harmful substances" are limited to illicit drugs. From a certain point of view, every individual is a drug user. Everyone has their own "drug of choice". For some, the "drug of choice" is commonly known and used, such as caffeine, nicotine, alcohol, or prescription drugs. For others, the "drug of choice" may be less commonly considered a drug, like television, movies, video games, religion, romance novels, work, love, sex, exercise, sleep, or food. Depending on the person, all of these things, along with illicit drugs, yield relief to the individual using them because of their effect on the dopamine system. This makes their use susceptible to addiction because of the elevated mood levels they generate. Almost all, however, produce diminishing satisfaction levels at large doses. It is important to know what drugs of choice one uses, for changes in the usage of one drug lead to alterations in the usage of others, so that homeostasis results.

Age is another factor that affects the dopamine system because the number of dopamine cells decreases by seven percent with every decade. For this reason, children have an easier time learning new things as they have more dopamine cells.

This fact may also partly account for the results of life happiness surveys. Results of these surveys usually show that extremes in emotions are more prevalent in the pre-adult stages of life. This might result from the decreasing number of dopamine cells, as well as having more direction in ones life. Additionally, if many things have already been learned, possible sources of reward diminish.

Now imagine that once again you are waiting to see your loved one after a long period of absence. Although your dopamine level surges at the moment you see the loved one, it increases with the mere anticipation of seeing the loved one again. In fact, every time you thought about the person your dopamine level probably rose to some extent. This partly explains why a state of excitement exists while you merely *wait* for a loved one. Your mind has been conditioned and is unconsciously regulating itself because of previous exposures to that particular stimulus—your loved one having previously induced this happy state—and therefore one need only imagine the stimulus to have a response. What if the stimulus was a bowl of homemade ice cream?

The phenomenon described above is known as the conditioned response and was discovered by a Russian physiologist named Ivan Pavlov in the early part of the twentieth century. At the time, Pavlov was interested in studying dog saliva, and at regular intervals he would go feed a group of dogs that he was using in his study. After a period of time, he noticed that the dogs would start to salivate when they saw him walk into the room. He reasoned that the dogs associated his presence in the room with the unconditioned stimulus, the food, so that his appearance was all that was necessary to make the dogs salivate; it alone evoked a new "conditioned" response (salivating).

Light and Dark

Another significant factor that plays a role in the physiological processes of almost all living organisms is the 24-hour cycle known as a circadian rhythm, based around the night-and-day cycle of the Earth. In humans and other animals, different brain chemicals are released on account of the presence or absence of light. One such brain chemical is melatonin, which serves to induce sleep by causing a drowsy state within the individual. Melatonin begins its release as the environment becomes darker, but subsides as it becomes brighter. When melatonin's production is not shut off completely within the system such as on an overcast day, a person's system remains in a depressed state, whereas on a sunny day, light shuts down the production of melatonin causing a more active state. The effect that light has on our brains is so instinctual that common culture has symbolized happiness with sunshine and sadness with rain and clouds.

Likewise, flowering plants will either not flower at all or not as effectively, if they are not provided with the appropriate night-and-day cycle. Even two minutes of light during the "night" cycle can harm a plant or even prevent flowering.

A perfect illustration of the effect light has on the nervous system can be seen in species of bears who live in temperate climates. When winter comes in this type of climate, bears not only become less active but go into a long hibernation, or period of greatly reduced activity. It is the internal mechanisms of the brain itself that control this behavior within the bear, due to the reduction of light during the winter months as well as several other factors.

Many people in colder, darker climates such as in Scandinavia, which has one of the world's highest suicide rates, experience a disorder known as Seasonal Affective Disorder, or SAD. SAD is caused by the extended hours of darkness and is depression that is caused by a lack of light. The usual treatment for SAD is exposing the individual to a sunlamp that emits all of the wavelengths present in regular sunlight, for a duration of 30 to 60 minutes per day. With this treatment, 80% of the individuals benefit to some degree, including 50% who fully recover from their SAD-induced depression.

Businesses take advantage of the effects of light by calculating the ideal brightness of the lights in their stores and offices so as to increase sales and productivity. Conversely, the "mood" lighting used in certain restaurants, and in any other venue trying to induce a romantic setting, helps achieve its purpose by inducing a feeling of isolation for a couple from the rest of the world, as well by neurologically inducing the minds to utilize their own calming chemicals.

Additionally and quite obviously, one's personality also plays a vast role in one's processing of information, thoughts, mood, and consciousness. Little is understood as to the physiology behind personality, as the psychological sciences understand only the basics at this time, but the effects of personality on the individual's world are immense. The effects of being either extroverted or introverted are prime examples. Extroverts tend to be more optimistic than introverts because human beings obtain many forms of happiness through social interaction. An introverted person, conversely, most likely sees things more pessimistically because the introvert is continually at odds with the world due to the fact that social interactions pose more of a challenge to them.

The sense of self, together with all of its implications, is so unconsciously ingrained in the mind that even amnesiacs, people who lost the ability to retrieve various parts of their memory, can still report what they are like. Even amnesiacs who have no recollection of anything that has occurred throughout their entire lives, including events that have just occurred but that are no longer in their short-term memory, are still able to say with a high degree of accuracy who they are. This seems to suggest that one's personality exists so strongly within one's being that it is detached, to a certain extent, from the events of one's past. It is internalized, and is therefore so much a part of the Self that everything that one experiences is completely colored by who one is.

The Self as Known

The other part of an individual's Self is the Self as Known—which, as mentioned earlier, comprises all of the elements impinging on the Self that are external to one's actual consciousness. The most influential of these elements is the body.

In many philosophies, the body is nothing more than a slave to the mind. As the Katha Upanishad puts it:

> Know the self as the lord of the chariot,
> the body as the chariot itself,
> the discriminating intellect as charioteer,

35

and the mind as the reins.
The senses, say the wise, are the horses;
Selfish desires are the roads they travel.

This implies the absolute indispensability of the mind, as the controller of the body, and the Self's existence and path.

But even though it is true that the mind is the source of the Self, controlling and shaping the body and one's actions, it is also true that the body controls and shapes the mind. To take an extreme example, imagine that the heart is no longer able to pump blood to the brain and therefore fuel the mind; lacking that fuel, the brain would die causing the mind's existence to cease. Consider, alternatively, the supermodel girl and the influence that her body has in shaping her Self because of the emphasis that society and she place upon her body; or the bodybuilder who is an abnormally strong human being with both him and others knowing it.

A person's body cannot help but exert a huge influence over who that person is and will become. In the nonhuman animal world, the bodies of individual animals play an essential role in determining who those animals will become within their own societies. In mate selection, it is usually the larger male that has superior access to the females. This is not only because their superior bodies enable them to attract mates easier and fend off other potential suitors, but also because their minds have adapted in response to how others perceive them. When an individual is larger than almost all of his peers, the other individuals will be more hesitant in approaching him. The mind of the dominant individual can't help but be influenced by his awareness of how his body influences others.

Now since the mind is more complex in humans than in animals, there exists a much more intricate interplay between mind and body. However, in the end, the basics still apply. The female supermodel, who is quite happily accustomed to others doing things for her, will internalize these experiences so that she sees the world as oriented to servicing her. The bodybuilder, who sees others cower in his presence, and who sees himself as a

36

massive individual with bulging muscles every time he looks in the mirror, internalizes such sights and becomes a more mentally dominant individual too. In fact, many who turn to weightlifting do so for this very purpose—to have the world, as they experience it, changed by altering the "vehicle" in which they travel through life.

One's current internal state at any given moment is also reflected in one's body. Some bodily states become habitual and are subsequently internalized within the mind, which in turn reinforces the habit. Imagine an individual who went through an emotionally debilitating experience and begins to slouch. Slouching, being easier for humans than standing straight, becomes a habit. This habit begins to influence the mind—not only on account of the actual feeling of slouching and being shorter, but also because of how others perceive the sloucher, as they treat him in a more demeaning manner conducive to his slouching position. A confident person, on the other hand, seems to reach toward the clouds as he faces the world, and will in turn cause others to look at him as they would look at a leader striding through a crowd. It is a natural instinct within the human mind to interpret others' social standing and current mental state by means of subconscious clues conveyed by others' bodies. The same subconscious effects also come into play with regards to short vs. tall people. Studies have shown that taller people are afforded more deference and are interpreted by others as being more powerful.

For these reasons and many more, it is imperative to realize the importance of one's body as an integral aspect of one's Self. To appreciate the body's effects upon the mind, and to understand that the mind exists only because of the body. When one eats, one provides their entire body, including their mind, with fuel with which to grow, to move, and to think. As discussed earlier, neurotransmitters are all composed of various elements which, if they are deficient in one's diet, may lead to the underperformance of one's body and mind.

Simone de Beauvoir illustrates this interplay between body and mind in her book, *The Second Sex*, when she describes

37

the effects of women's more irregular heartbeat. She explains that due to this irregular heartbeat, the female mind is in *flux* to a greater extent than the male mind. Women accordingly experience a more rapidly evolving emotional state, which could make their understanding of their emotions more difficult and could partly explain why women are more prone to depression.

Now imagine that an affliction such as a viral infection or a broken bone has gripped the body. To the extent that the pain and discomfort are significant, the mind becomes affected. The outside world appears a little darker depending on the strength of the debilitating condition, and the individual's thoughts are thus altered.

It is important to realize, however, that the body itself manifests to one's Self as nothing more than electrochemical signals in the brain. The body may be seen, it may be felt, heard, smelt, and even tasted but all of these sensations ultimately are only known via the brain. The body is *perceived*, not known. As with all perceived entities, it can be blocked out to a certain extent and overcome by the mind.

Though it may seem contrary to ordinary thought, the Self can be viewed as determined in part by entities existing beyond the boundaries of one's body and mind. Social relations are one example. Ever heard of the expression "You are whom you are friends with"? This adage, though obviously not entirely correct, shows how intricately social relations are involved in the formation of one's Self. For when a person is around different people, he or she has different Selves. For instance, consider how you would talk to the following people: to a police officer who has just stopped you for speeding? To a member of the opposite sex at a bar? To your mother, father, brother, or sister? To a person much older or younger than you?

It has been often said that one has as many Selves as one has social relations. It is inevitable that one is more likely to talk about politics with a journalist and about Pokémon with your child. Imagine if you reversed this pattern. The journalist might be slightly amused, and your child would probably fall asleep.

People often like to meet someone who is completely

different from anyone else they have ever met, for the very reason that such a person brings out features in themselves that had lain dormant or unexpressed. However, people also often like to meet people very similar to their self. An explanation for these affinities seems to be offered in the Hindu text, the Upanishads:

> *You love your spouse because of the Self;*
> *You love your sibling because of the Self;*
> *You love your friend because of the Self.*

Simply stated, many relationships exist because one sees oneself, or who one would like to be in some way, in another person, which serves as a form of self-validation or inspiration. It is as if the individual briefly achieves a sense of freedom from the eternal isolation of one's own being by seeing oneself, or part of oneself, in another. It is partly for this reason that when a loved one dies, a part of oneself dies as well.

The Self, especially under the capitalist system, also includes one's material possessions: the clothes on one's back, one's car, the food one eats, the music one listens to at home. How could this not be so? For you are affected both by your "stuff" and by how others perceive you with, or in relation to, your stuff.

Imagine an individual driving down the street in a brand-new Ferrari. Others turn their heads and stare. Whether they stare at the car or the person does not matter, for the effect will be the same on the individual. Even if a destitute individual were in the passenger seat, people would still look at the person as if he were a celebrity, as if he had money. This deference afforded the driver or passenger would in most cases have a considerable impact upon the driver and his perception of himself. Stepping into a vehicle that can go from zero to 60 miles per hour in 3 seconds gives a person a completely different outlook. After all, he can go faster than anything else around him, and many people look at him when he drives by. Maybe he himself thinks that he is faster, more beautiful, or more important. The only others who receive such treatment, after all, are celebrities and heads of state.

In a way however, driving a Ferrari may begin to influence a person in such a way as to actually make the thoughts about himself derived from driving the car true. The Ferrari, along with people's reactions to the person and the car, may make the driver want to dress more nicely, for example, because people are looking at him. The car thus transfers a little bit of itself to the person. Negative attributes would undoubtedly be transferred as well: extravagance, superficiality, and arrogance, to name a few.

Another major source of the formation of the Self are labels you and others place upon yourself. What are you? "I'm a liberal." "I'm a conservative." "A chemist." "An economist." "I'm nice." "I'm arrogant." Even "labels" that can not help but be part of ones self such as, man or woman, act as labels in so much as the individual plays the societal stereotypes of each one respectively.

Each one of these labels and the many others like them immediately give one a sense of who they are in the world. If one says she is "a liberal," the stereotypes surrounding being a liberal, though not originally part of the person, will slowly become true of the person after a period of time. For example, let us assume that this person has a couple of very strong liberal beliefs that exist from the person's own ruminations, but does not really believe strongly in any other stereotypical liberal stances. Now, because she feels so strongly about a couple of liberal beliefs, she votes for liberal candidates. By supporting these candidates, she has automatically aligned herself liberally with the other liberal topics that these candidates support.

Gradually, and for a number of reasons, the liberal stances for the topics of lesser importance to her will likely become her stances too in order that she support her candidate, or ally, who fights for the beliefs that really do matter to her. Of equal impact, is the mind's natural inclination towards self-consistency. By voting for the candidate, she voted for all of the things that the candidate is for as well. To reconcile any inconsistencies existing between her own thought and that of the candidates, she will expend less energy by simply adopting all of the candidate's views. This is particularly true since free time is a luxury to most people.

Though essentially impossible to avoid, being labeled influences your mind to an often alarming extent. People will, often quite unfortunately, let these labels of who they are dictate their decisions and beliefs unthinkingly. In such cases, the label has become part of the individual's Self. The individual becomes a mere "robot," subject to the programming given him or her by the label and what it conveys to society. Lazy minds succumb quickly to such programming, without even knowing that they are doing so.

Perception

The word "perception" refers to what we apprehend of the physical world from our five senses. The five known senses that human beings have are sight, hearing, smell, touch, and taste. Each of these senses is used to varying degrees in different individuals, with the sense of sight dominating most human beings' perceptual experience of the world.

It is extremely important, however, to realize that perception does not equal reality; perception only equals one's *perceived* reality. If, for instance, you actually believe that on a sunny day the sky is blue, you have been fooled by your mind. The sky has no "color"; it is merely composed of a mixture of various elements that reflect the electromagnetic wavelengths from the sun's light. These wavelengths do not hold any color within themselves, just as the infrared waves given off by your own body do not.

Now, if you were one of several heat-sensing snakes, you might be able to sense the infrared waves emitted from objects in your environment, such as a warm blooded mouse, by one of several pits embedded just above your mouth. Because of the way our species developed, we do not sense most infrared waves except for the longer wavelength ones, known as far infrared waves, which we sense as heat via temperature-sensitive nerve

41

endings in the skin. We are, however, one of a very few species of mammals that can perceive portion of the electromagnetic spectrum known as the visible spectrum as color. We are able to discern color because of cells on the retina, at the back of the eye, called cones, which react chemically to light (rods being the other set of photoreceptors, which sense intensity of light).

Color in itself, however, does not exist in the world—only in our minds. Our perceptual system, which filters all visible stimuli from the outside world, takes the information from the wavelengths that pass through our minds and turns it into images that we can "see" inside of our brains.

It is much like a computer, where an image of a blue box may be encoded in binary language (e.g., 0011100101). Now, suppose that "0011100101" actually did represent a blue box in computer language and was stored on a CD-Rom. "0011100101" itself is colorless and shapeless, and exists only in a digital format burned onto the CD, where it would not be visible to the naked eye as a blue box. Nevertheless, when the CD is placed into the CD-Rom player of a computer, a three-dimensional looking blue box becomes visible to the human perceptual system on the computer screen.

In other words, because of limitations within our own perceptual system we were unable to see that a blue box was in front of our eyes all along. For surely, even though our eyes, ears, nose, touch sensors, and taste-buds were unable to sense the blue box, the computer, equipped with entirely different sensory equipment specifically built to detect and translate the pits on CDs, was perfectly able to detect the blue box. It then translated from the information on the CD-Rom into what we could perceive as a blue box visually.

Knowing the strengths and weaknesses of our human perceptual system allows us not to be deceived by our minds, thereby enabling knowledge to enter the mind a little less obscured. It helps to keep the mind open to possibilities that may not be immediately perceivable. An ignorant mind may pass by the subtlest of items and miss something of extreme importance, owing to a fixed belief that one's perception equals reality.

To take an example, have you ever noticed the way some stars in the sky seem to disappear when looked at directly? This is because of the intricacies of your eyes, which have developed, like almost everything in nature, with utmost economy and purpose. For although one may not realize it, owing to naturally growing up with the vision one has, only a small portion of one's vision is actually in focus at any one time. This is because the eye has the highest concentration of cones right next to the very center of the retina, in a section known as the fovea. Outside of the fovea, rods predominate. Now cones may be more evolutionarily advanced, making possible perception of vivid color and focused imagery, but rods allow one to see at lower-intensity light levels. Therefore it is difficult to see some stars clearly at night, because their light emissions are too low-intensity to be captured by the cones located in the center of your vision, and are able to be picked up only by the rods, at the edges of one's vision.

The senses can also be obscured by one's internal state. In such instances, however, the problem lies not with the perceptual system itself, but with the thought processes through which external stimuli pass. In such circumstances—such as when one is having a bad day—everything seems darker and dulled. People may appear hostile or apathetic; children may no longer seem cute and innocent, but rather resemble raging monsters. But when the clouds of your mind clear, everything seems to be a little bit better than it actually is, leading to distorted beliefs about the world in the opposite direction.

Imagine that suddenly, while reading this book, you lost all of your senses. You could no longer see a spring morning—just blackness. You could no longer hear the soft whistle of a passing wind—just silence. You could no longer feel the dewy grass—or, for that matter, your body. No more of the sweet smell of going by a bakery. No more tasting your mother's freshly baked cookies. No sense of the external world at all.

Who would you consider yourself to be? To yourself, you have no image, no voice, no smell; no feel to your skin and body; no taste when sweat catches the side of your mouth. You would exist only as your thoughts. As Descartes said, "I think, therefore I am." It is your thoughts, contained within your ephemeral consciousness, that ultimately define who you are.

Now open your eyes. But do not just open them; *open* them—to the fact that millions of sensations, filtered through all five limited senses, are constantly streaming through your mind at any one given moment, with only a few ever being attended to by one's consciousness.

Right now, my fingers are gently rapping against a keyboard. Little black lines scrawl across a lit screen. The gentle sounds of Pachelbel's Canon are playing in the background. There is a slight remnant taste of the tea I had just gently washed down my throat, and a warmness in my chest and throat from the tea. A fuzzy desk and fuzzy notebooks appear just outside of my eyes' focusing point. And there are other sensations. The hum of trains running along nearby tracks. The whirling of my hard drive. The smell of my neighbor's Moroccan cooking. My gluteus maximus pressed firmly by gravity against the chair I'm sitting on.

The basis for understanding perception is understanding that what we perceive through our senses is only what our senses and mind *allow* us to perceive. Your perception, which is the means by which you understand anything about this world, comprises:

> - *vision as if you saw through foggy lenses.*
> - *hearing as if you always wore earmuffs.*
> - *smell as if you were all the time in a musty room.*
> - *touch as if you always wore gloves.*
> - *taste as if your mouth was already tainted with another flavor.*

Information abounds in the world. One just has to know how and through what filters one receives it. Our senses may limit us to a certain extent, but the mind that is aware of its limitations can always conquer them, with dedication and imagination. Knowledge is the ability to transcend. To understand everything, one must understand through what filters one is *sensing* everything.

Putting It All Together

The mind is the most incredible and important tool you use in life. It at once reveals the Self, as you are aware of it, and the outside world, as you experience *it*. It allows you the ability to think and at the same time controls your thoughts. It defines the very essence of who you are, for you would not exist without consciousness, and at the same time conveys an illusion of a world that seems so real that you can hardly conceive of the "true" physical world.

The foundation for all your knowledge—and, therefore, for the knowledge of all things—is your Self and thus your mind. An untamed mind is much like a mischievous being that is constantly implanting illusions inside one's mind, making one believe "A" when "B" may be closer to the truth.

The untamed mind thrives on biases, which can arise from such things as emotions and labels—or just laziness. To understand all things, on the other hand, mastery of the mind is required. Mastery of the mind is like mastery of the controls of anything. In order to have utmost control, one must understand the item to be controlled to the utmost. However, no person is completely in control of his or her mind; there are just far too many stimuli to wade through. The Bhagavad Gita says that one needs to strive to peel the layers of ignorance away from the "god" inside one—one's mind.

Acceptance of who you are in ways that you are unable to change is critical, for desire with no possible chance of satisfaction is likely only to lead the mind astray on fruitless chases that cloud judgment. Although there are many things that one has no control over, you are given a mind to control, however intractable it may be. The world is filled with lies and liars, but the biggest liar is often oneself. Without self-knowledge, one can never truly understand anything.

45

II.

Divisions and Classifications...

the breaking up of the whole.

"Time has no divisions to mark its passage, there is never a thunderstorm or blare of trumpets to announce the beginning of a new month or year. Even when a new century begins it is only we mortals who ring bells and fire off pistols."

- *Thomas Mann*

DIVISIONS & CLASSIFICATIONS are for mortals; the whole is for the gods. For what if one were to become a god? How much would you be able to perceive and know at any one given moment in time? What if you could know everything that was going on in Los Angeles, London, Delhi, and Tokyo all at the same time; for that matter, what about everywhere else, including what's occurring beneath your feet in the Earth's core as well as the exact position of every single atom in the universe?

Of course, human beings with our current knowledge and technology cannot even begin to approach such abilities. Some studies suggest that human beings are able to concentrate on only one stimulus, whether it is external or internal, at any particular moment. Now you may be thinking, "I'm aware of much more than one stimulus at a time," and in a way you would be correct, for our consciousness takes in several items at any one time. However, it is believed that even if you have six items in your consciousness that are almost immediately retrievable, your focused attention can be directed to only one of these items.

For example, try to think of a square and a circle at the same time. Notice that although you have the conception of both a square and a circle in your mind, in order to perceive both of them, your mind has to quickly switch back and forth between them. At any given moment, both cannot exist within your mind.

Schizophrenics' fundamental problem arises from the fact that their minds switch back and forth between items in their consciousness in a much too rapid and uncontrolled manner. Conversations with schizophrenics are usually marked by very abrupt changes in the topic of conversation. Schizophrenics also have a poor memory because of the difficulty they have in keeping thoughts in their consciousness long enough to place them into long-term memory.

Although I will not describe the details of the neurological basis for what causes these impairments in schizophrenics, the major source of their attention deficit is an abnormally high level of dopamine in certain sections of the brain. Certain drugs induce similar effects by raising the levels of dopamine in the brain, causing such side effects as memory deficits, laughter at inappropriate moments, along with a higher degree of artistic awareness. This artistic awareness—as in schizophrenics, who tend to have a somewhat similar cognition to that of artists—may be a result of uncontrolled attention, enabling the comparison of various items in their brains that normally would not be compared. Likewise, Jacob Bronowski defined the creative act as uncovering hidden likenesses between seemingly disparate things or ideas.

The average individual, however, possesses a much more controlled attention-directing brain. The human brain, like the brains of almost all other animals, has developed through environmental forces to enable humans to recognize and distinguish between stimuli in order to be better equipped to survive in this world. For example, the necessity of obtaining

48

food is aided by the brain's controlled attention, as would be necessary when hunting a deer or avoiding predation.

Although the ability of the brain to divide and classify stimuli has been and continues to be absolutely necessary and beneficial for human survival, as with any strength there is a corresponding weakness. Entrenched with divisions and classifications, the brain is unable to see the similarities existing between the things that it divides and classifies, resulting in a more limited grasp of knowledge and an overall incomplete worldview. This incompleteness of thought is increasingly maladaptive in today's "global" society, in which information is vital to success.

Evolutionarily Created

When the first single-celled autotrophic (i.e. energy-producing), asexual (i.e. self-replicating) organisms developed on this planet, the first element needed for survival was an inhabitable environment. These first organisms probably exhibited a simple stimulus-response system which allowed them to "seek" out environments with the proper temperature and chemical makeup.

However, through the evolution of these organisms, new species arose that were heterotrophic—acquiring energy through the consumption of other organisms—and sexual. These two new survival mechanisms added additional complexity to organisms as not only do they need to find inhabitable environments, but also food, mates and protection from predators.

By the time the first humans arrived, the complexity of organisms on the planet had become much greater. Vertebrate animals developed a complex stimulus-response system largely focused around the nervous system, composed of the spinal cord, nerves, and the brain. This system gave these organisms the ability to instinctually divide the world up into categories in ways that were necessary for the species' survival. For example, an organism had to be able to recognize that if it was going to eat, it had to eat edible red berries, not poisonous black ones. It needed

49

to find a mate of the opposite anatomy and defend it from others of the same anatomy.

At this period in human development, human beings were not concerned with the characteristics of the whole as much as they were with the details of the specific, as survival was the focus Of course, this is not to state that early humans did not have any conception of the whole; they probably did to a limited extent.

The advent of agriculture and the domestication of animals, first prominently seen in Egypt and sections of the Middle East, enabled the once nomadic human to live in one place. Human beings now developed societies in which they specialized with respect to their labor. Up until this point, the most prominent display of specialization among human labor existed probably between the men and women of nomadic bands as well as within the overall hierarchical structure between young and old.

The polytheistic religious belief systems of many of the great early civilizations conceived of many gods, in an almost natural response to their being at the mercy of many different elements. These religious systems fulfilled deeper psychological needs than just the need for survival. The mysteriousness of death had to be explained to an ever increasingly advanced society whose basic needs were much better met.. Human beings needed a system with which to understand death so that they may be comforted. These early enclaves into what would become modern religion can be seen to represent the beginning of peoples' search for an understanding of the whole as their understanding of the parts increased. Additionally, the fact that most early religious systems were polytheistic seems to show an evolution of human thought where in today's world the majority of people now follow monotheistic religions. The one time gods of polytheism have in many instances been replaced through scientific explanations of naturally occurring phenomenon.

One of the first civilizations, the polytheistic Egyptians, began the practice of embalming, or preserving, their leaders' bodies after death in order that their leaders would attain the realm of the gods. They would also preserve everything alongside the pharaoh's corpse, from his internal organs to his personal servants, for use in the next life. These burial practices, though not the first, were the some of the most complex. Their complexity indicates the emphasis that people now began to give to non-survival based activities and thought.

In eastern Asia, a religious belief system known as Taoism began around 1500 B.C. Taoism did not divide the world up into easily understandable parts, but rather focused on the whole. Its understanding of the world was based upon the idea that opposites existed everywhere and that the combination of these constantly cycling opposites represented something larger and indescribable: the Whole. The teachings found in Taoism are exceptionally similar to today's chaos theory, which expresses a belief in simplicity within complexity. This simplicity makes the complex easier to understand; the whole is understood through its parts. Because everything is related, everything can be understood.

Next, during the so-called Classical Age of the ancient Western world centered around Greece, there was an increasing prevalence of divisions and classifications as cities began becoming ever more complex. However, at the same time, scholars were still rarely ever anything more than philosophers who would study all subject matter. The great Greek philosophers of this time, including Socrates, Plato, and Aristotle, studied everything from mathematics and biology to morality and literature. Even the *word* philosophy means simply, "the love of knowledge," indicating no distinctions within the knowledge that one sought. This was a period of great growth and development. This period's writings would eventually serve to bring the Western World out of the Dark Ages well over a millennia later and act as the basis for modern thought and knowledge.

The Greeks' fascination with the "perfection" of mathematics led them to apply the principles of mathematics to other things. For example, they sought to construct a moral and political system based upon the same idealistic principles as the perfect circle or square. They believed that such a governing system might be as perfect as the geometric shapes they studied, thereby indicating a belief in the interrelatedness of many things in the world and further showing their advanced understanding of the whole.

After the fall of the Roman Empire, 476 A.D., however, the centers of Western civilization collapsed back into despotism, with many of the writings of this new era coming from members of the church who were society's philosophers, studying the ancient texts particularly with regard to their religious implications. Unlike the ancient philosophers, who were really the forerunners of modern scientists, these theologians generally studied with a very specific intent of relating their studies to God and the Bible. Although they may have studied many things, they had a narrow-minded focus and society suffered.

During the so-called Renaissance of the 15th century, a revival of interest was spawned in the works from before the fall of Rome, 476AD, among people outside of the church. Knowledge for its own sake, instead of its relation to church dogma, was sought. During this time period in 1452, Leonardo Da Vinci was born. Today, his name invokes images of paintings, blue prints for flying machines, philosophy, studies of human physiology, the nature of light, as well as a whole host of other endeavors. This breadth of knowledge and skill-sets of his and many other people of this time would eventually coin the term, Renaissance man, as someone who did a lot of different things. Specialization, for the most part among the academic world, had not arisen yet.

In 1637, Descartes, considered the father of modern philosophy and who himself was an academic of many disciplines, published his, *Discourse on the Method*, helping to lay the foundation for the modern world by providing a sort of methodology as to how investigations of science should be conducted. Over the next 200 years, specialization of knowledge proliferated at an unprecedented rate, especially within the industrialized societies that were being created. People no longer would be acclaimed "Renaissance men," but instead would become biologists, physicists, mathematicians; philosophers or psychologists; economists or physiologists or artists. Specialization was an inevitable process that would be spawned from better communications and a general increase in knowledge.

In 1776, Adam Smith, who wrote *The Wealth of Nations,* which many consider to be the foundation of modern economics, championed the concept of division of labor as an economically important principle for increasing output while decreasing cost. In line with this principle, specialized companies arose with the sole purpose of outputting one particular item or group of items. Smith's work, along with then recent developments in technology, helped spawn the Industrial Revolution, which vastly increased economic output and increased specialization in the workforce to ever higher degrees. Specialization's time had come.

At the beginning of the 20th century, Henry Ford, founder of the Ford Motor Company, borrowed the notion of the assembly line from a smaller company that specialized in refrigerated rail cars. He started to produce the Model T to the exclusion to any other model (the principle of comparative advantage) and employed people on an assembly line, where their job would consist of doing the same thing over and over again throughout their shift (division of labor). This, of course, vastly increased productivity, because employing specialists—having many workers finely tuned to do one task (for example, installing power converters into an engine)—enabled them to do that one task faster than people who would, at another car company, build the whole engine by themselves. This efficiency allowed Ford significantly undercut the competition's prices. As Ford said, "There is one rule for the industrialist and that is: Make the best quality of goods possible at the lowest cost possible, paying the highest wages possible."

This tradition lives on today with divisions and classifications more evident than ever before. When one gets an upper-level degree from a university, it may be in something as specialized as nuclear physics, Asian-American studies, Italian cinema, Irish literature, molecular biology, or the anthropology of the Incas. Similarly, people are not simply Christians, but identify with one of over 20,000 Christian sects, each with its' own slightly differing biblical or theological interpretation and manner of conducting worship. Fast food is no longer a burger, fries, and a shake, but instead may be a steak, onion, lettuce, and rice burrito; a club sandwich with Swiss cheese on a toasted sourdough roll; or a chicken chow mein, beef broccoli, and sweet-and-sour pork combination plate.

There are so many divisions and classifications today that in order for one to become an "expert" at anything, one has to study for years in large part just to learn the jargon that characterizes each particular area of knowledge. Furthermore, with the globalization of our world, so many cultures have become intertwined with other cultures in a myriad of ways, from music and popular culture to literature and cuisine. This complexity existing within the world is one of the largest contributors to the formation of divisions and classifications, for we must navigate an incomprehensibly complex world with limited-capacity minds. According to Norbert Wiener, who wrote, in the original introduction to his *Cybernetics*, that Leibniz, in the eighteenth century, was perhaps the last man "who . . . had a full command of all the intellectual activity of his day." The only possible means of even beginning to grasp the world in general is to examine one piece of it at a time.

The Effects of Divisions and Classifications

It has been said that a newborn baby is at its peak of openness. It may be male or female, white or black, but it has not yet chosen who it is. Even given one's parents' genetic makeup, which plays a large role in the formation of an individual, a newborn still can be molded. It has not yet started down a particular path and can still to a certain extent be led down any path presented to it.

In Taoist philosophy, it is said that one should always strive to be like a newborn. People should try to free their minds from their conditioning and biases in order that what they perceive will be closer to the truth. Fixation of the mind, in the form of already established thoughts, perspectives, and beliefs, causes the flow of information to become diverted as if by rocks within a river.

Preconceived notions are perhaps the greatest negative consequence of divisions and classifications. The inability of people who are set in a particular way to see other possibilities as potentially equally valid causes such individuals to become blind to the truth, and to knowledge of other thought systems. The closed mind arises because the mind is fixated on one particular division or classification within the world such as one academic discipline, religion, or overall mental state. Conversely, the fluid, open mind has the ability, like water, to take on many forms in its continual adaptation to different situations in its attempt to understand the world around it.

An entrepreneur with very limited resources, for example, will have to "wear many hats," within their venture, the fluidity with which they are able to change hats often determining their success. Many cognitive frameworks will be necessary for them to effectively launch their company. The mathematical/business framework will have to become salient when they are working on budgeting or attempting to figure out which loan provides the best long-term outcome. The artistic framework will have to become salient when working on the marketing and advertising. The technical framework will arise when they are engineering and building their company's product. Many start-up companies fail because the entrepreneur was really interested in one thing while all of the other areas were neglected. The picture of the whole company becomes either ignored or distorted.

Now, look at the issue of race relations. The truth of the matter is that this should not even be an issue. People are people. Ones disposition or worth is not a matter of race but rather ones actions. In theory, of course, this works perfectly well; in practice, however, it is hard to overcome the basic psychology of the mind, which has evolved to ensure survival through the use of divisions and classifications whose natural byproduct is racism.

Take, for example, a black child, whose parents are open-minded and who at this point in his life has never had any negative experiences with anyone of any other race. Now, unless his friends are bigoted, he probably has no real negative feelings toward other races, except possibly as acquired through media. At the age of nine years old, however, he is brutally attacked by a white man, who has no ulterior motive other than to harm him because he is black.

This child, who is at such a young and impressionable age, will remember this incident for the rest of his life; his or her brain has been forever altered. Years later, walking down the street, he notices a white man approaching him from the other direction. How is he going to "read" this man? It is difficult to imagine that he could not help but think negative thoughts in regards to this man, because of the negative previous experience that he had with another white man. After he was assaulted, a negative loop was established whereby he gradually began to color everything white people said or did in a more negative light, leading him to respond in a generally worse fashion to all whites. This is simply instinct—the brain's mechanism to ensure our survival as living beings.

But imagine how such fears—and, conversely, likes— affect such an individual's ability to think. Whenever he now sees a white man, he is immediately biased by his previous experience. He has classified (even if unconsciously) white men as dangerous. A biased individual encounters the other no longer as a particular individual but as an agglomeration of all other, similar individuals that he has come across before. For surely an open, friendly white man poses little threat to a black man, but the internal mechanisms of the brain will not allow the individual to see the truth of the current reality on account of his past experiences.

One of the greatest divisive entities that is and has been a cause of much of the world's conflict is religion. For the most part, with a very few exceptions, having faith in one religion excludes for the possibility of having faith in another either out of dogma or practice. Religion divides the world up between us and them, black and white, right and wrong.

Its divisive influences could only be said to be matched

by the strength that it gathers from its dealings with death. The fate of our very own mortality is at risk with any discussion that includes religion, for each religion has its own answers as to how to achieve immortality or lasting peace. Fear is one of if not *the* largest contributing factors for religion's existence. The fear of the unknown that follows the death of our human bodies has very large both conscious and unconscious psychological implications in our minds. Ignorance and fear causes people to attack that which is not understood or that which is feared, whether it is a harmless snake or an entire country. One only needs to look at history to see the number of wars fought for or in part due to religion.

Academia is another fertile example of divisions and classifications. It is an arena where many people have devoted their entire professional lives studying and or teaching one discipline. Getting even more focused, they do not just study and teach one discipline but a section of that discipline. With such devotion it's difficult to imagine how their minds could not be dramatically influenced by their narrowly defined areas of study. This special relationship seems likely to cause biased views from the academic's own desires to be important as well as from an overall fondness for the discipline.

The age-old division of the sexes is another perfect example. How can it be said that either sex is superior to the other when neither could exist without the other? How can any entity be superior to another when its existence depends upon that other? Without either sex, the human race would have died long ago. No advancement would have taken place if procreation of the species had not occurred, and procreation can, obviously, happen only with the participation of both sexes. Even when women were still expected to stay at home to raise children while the men were off fighting wars or working at some trade, both roles were important and absolutely vital to the success of the society as a whole. How can one even begin to quantify the importance of one division and classification vis-à-vis another when the two are intricately linked? Rather, each has its advantages, and each its disadvantages.

The most devastating result of divisions and classifications is war. War arises because the perceived divisions existing between two entities become so great as to draw them into mortal combat. One does not attempt to kill another that is perceived to be similar unless of course the assailant also dislikes their self. People who seem to be similar to us even just superficially are perceived to hold the same values and desires for the future. This lack of friction or antagonism yields a very low probability for conflict. The act of War is possible only because of antagonisms in large part due to divisions and classifications.

The opposite of war is peace, and if hate is a factor in war then love could be considered to be a factor in peace. Now, in our world that seems destined to forever exist in varying shades of grey, if two countries are at war or peace, they do not necessarily hate or love each other. For that matter, war and particularly peace themselves are in many ways matters which are not always clear cut. For example, a country can place sanctions upon another country in order to influence it by harming them economically. Such sanctions can prove extremely devastating to the country harming it, just as a war would, except without using physical force. The Cold War is another example of animosities existing between two countries that are at peace where both sides tried to harm the other without actually directly firing a shot.

In any case, love as with peace exists as a conception of an "idealized" state that rarely if ever exists in its ultimate sense because the world is always in some form of conflict. As Plato said, "Only the dead have seen the end of war." Perhaps it is this conflict that causes love to be held up so high by humanity. The desire for love in its highest state where divisions seem to disappear as the other person becomes a sort of extension of one self. As Freud said, "a man who is in love declares that 'I' and 'you' are one." Love, in direct contrast to hate and war, creates a whole instead of the splintering of one, as it builds one from two.

However, despite the negatives that result from divisions and classifications, the human race in general would be nowhere near where it is today without the many divisions and classifications that exist. One example of the advantages of divisions and classifications is the Ford Motor Company's success at the beginning of the twentieth century when they put into operation the first large-scale use of the assembly line. Because of the division of labor among many individuals, each worker was able to perfect his ability to work on building one part of a whole car instead of the whole thing. This new practice increased production exponentially and enabled Ford to dominate the car market for over a decade due to its low prices which the average person could afford.

Specialization dominates our society today, and our level of specialization is, in fact, necessary for the continued growth of knowledge and technology. It increases peoples' comparative advantage in the areas in which they specialize, enabling them to conserve resources and delve deeper into specific areas of knowledge. The resulting discoveries can be of immense benefit to the general population.

Divisions also serve as a means to organize thoughts into manageable structures that can be understood and worked with easier. For example, imagine the periodic table, which lists elements, from top to bottom, by the number of neutrons in their respective atoms' cores. The main difference at a subatomic level of these elements is their varying amounts of protons, neutrons, and electrons. These variations are what give them their unique properties. Dmitri Mendeleev, the accredited inventor of the modern periodic table, divided these elements into columns of elements that held similar properties. As one goes from left to right on the table, the elements go from metals to non-metals. By dividing these elements up and displaying them on the periodic table, the practice of chemistry becomes exceptionally easier.

Moreover, complex communication—or, in fact, any form of communication—would be impossible if it was not for divisions and classifications. When one tries to express anything, one makes use of the commonly known divisions and classifications that have been assigned to entities in the world in the form of symbols, names, or vocal utterances. The very reason that communication works is because of the assigned meanings that certain visual and verbal symbols possess which can then be deciphered by others who know that particular language. If all words were assumed to mean the same thing, conveyance of information would be impossible. For that matter, divisions and classifications also allow human beings and other animals to decipher to a certain extent what other beings' current mental states by their body language and facial expressions. Babies instinctually are able to understand these non-verbal cues showing the brain's innate ability to divide up the world.

To take an abstract example, imagine if one was to find a point on a circle. If one was only aware of the whole, the point would disappear into the circle. Likewise, if one were to try to find a circle and could only see a series of points, the circle itself would evade the individual's consciousness.

Being able to see the whole while taking note of the divisions and classifications that exist allows for a free-flowing perspective that is flexible enough to be in accord with a reality close to the truth. For whenever a line is drawn, two sides form out of what was once and still is one. The division and the corresponding labels have made it two.

Putting It All Together

As with anything else, divisions and classifications have as many bad elements as good. For although they allow one to function within this world with the brain that we were given, they can also create a narrow-minded perspective through which one sees the world. For example, a liberal may not see the validity in some conservative beliefs which may actually benefit a country, and vice versa. Each has allowed their beliefs, their part of the world's ideological whole, to overwhelm other possible beliefs.

A world without divisions and classifications, however, is far from an acceptable solution to the problems that divisions and classifications bring about. Within religion itself, numerous observations have been made regarding human beings' inability to deal with the whole. One such example occurs when Moses ascends Mount Sinai to receive the Ten Commandments from God. Before he reaches the top, an angel appears before Moses and tells him that no man can look upon God, and that the result of even a glimpse of Him would be death. God supposedly existing everywhere and knowing all things is too much for a human being to handle, not being equipped with the capabilities to exist as a whole.

The duality between divisions and classifications and the whole is very similar to the duality between knowledge and thought. For knowledge exists only as long as thought exists— just as divisions and classifications depend on the existence of the whole. Contrariwise, thought exists only as long as knowledge and the existence of the whole depends on there being divisions and classifications.

Knowledge is a necessary contingency for thought to exist. For if one had no knowledge, including knowledge of oneself, the world, and thought itself, how could one think? Knowledge is the foundation from which thought exists and derives more knowledge.

It is important to be aware of the divisions and classifications that break up the world in which we live, which is nothing more than a whole seen by our senses and brain as comprised of many parts. Divisions and classifications are not something to break free of—only, rather, to recognize as artificial elements that can be utilized by the mind. After all, our brains function on the basis of divisions and classifications: Food is good; pain is bad.

Recognition of the whole will undoubtedly increase in the so-called Information Age, where information of any sort is only a click of a mouse away. For more knowledge equals greater understanding. Without recognition of the whole in an age where the world teeters precariously with regard to its very survival— owing to many issues, ranging from nuclear weapons to environmental damage—globally devastating effects could be imminent. We are all connected, for the air we breathe was once a tree, which was once a human being, which was once a loaf of bread, and which was once part of the heavens above.

III.

Systems...
& the many within.

"Who sees with equal eye, as God of all,
A hero perish or a sparrow fall,
Atoms or systems into ruin hurl'd,
And now a bubble burst, and now a world."

- Alexander Pope

"The SYSTEM," as defined by this book, is everything existing within the universe, from atoms and galaxies to this book and you, the reader. This is the overall System, and it is comprised of an infinite number of smaller ones.

Now, the word "system" has become quite popular. It seems as if everyone is always talking about this or that system, whether it be systems dedicated to weight loss or ones used to manage companies. The word has been used so much that its power and original meaning seem to be in danger of becoming diluted.

A definition for "systems", as defined by Michael Gerber, author of the E-myth series of books, is:

A system is a set of things, actions, ideas, and information that interact with each other, and in so doing, alter other systems.

Using this definition, however, it seems that anything could be called a system. This is actually true, for a system exists between any two entities, independent of their size or essence. It therefore may seem simplistic or even redundant to delve into systems any further, but that would be ignoring the huge power that this simplicity holds in dealing with something as complex as the world existing around us. It is crucial to understand systems— for each system, as shown in the succeeding chapters, has certain characteristics that, if known, yield information previously unknown about our world.

Additionally, knowledge of one system provides knowledge of another, for everything exists within the System and therefore is bound to its particular rules or tendencies. Everything that exists within the System ultimately will be forced to adapt to it. The adaptations that take place are dependent upon the unique characteristics of each independent entity and their respective sub-systems; three simple ones for Earth being: air, water, and land. However, the overall laws pertaining to these are the same; all are subjugated to Newton's Laws of Motion.

It is important, in thinking about systems, to realize that they exist as nothing more than human-created constructs, created by people to help them understand the world and its various connections so as to be able to better predict and control it. In essence systems really do not exist except in the minds of people, for the world just *is*, and does not know or need to know the various relationships among its parts. However, inasmuch as systems do exist only in the mind, it is important, in thinking about systems, for one's mind to be relaxed, and for it to be allowed to stray. As systems themselves are not in any strict sense contained, owing to the multitude and interconnectivity of systems, the mind that tries to understand them must not be contained either, except only occasionally.

As discussed in the last chapter, the idea of the Whole is incomprehensible, and that is why there exist divisions and classifications, which make understanding the Whole easier. The following discussion will attempt to enhance our understanding further through the categories of "micro" and "macro" systems. Both terms are merely arbitrary labels that provide a way to break down and organize the incomprehensible number of systems that exist, making it easier to think about them and about the overall System.

Microsystems

Systems come in many varieties, including small. For size, as with everything else, is relative. What is small to the human being is gigantic to the ant. Do you remember, as a child, that one item that you had, in my case a jacket, that seemed so large? Often that item, revisited after many years, no longer seems large but in fact has become small.

Let's examine some of the microsystems that exist. Atoms exist as a system with negatively charged electrons in an outer core, orbiting a positively charged center composed of protons and neutrons. Each element within this system affects the system in a unique manner; each allows the system itself to exist. If just one of the protons within the nucleus were removed, for example, the atom's properties would change and the atom itself would become the atom of a different element. The opposing electrical charges keep the system intact, with the electrons kept in place by the protons and the protons by the electrons. Both of these subatomic particles exist in relation to the other within that system.

A cashier and a customer exist as a system within the overall economic system of a country and the world. The cashier exists to operate the cash register while the customer exists to purchase various items from the cashier. If no one paid for goods, the need for a cashier would disappear as was the case when bartering was more common. Today, however, with Internet commerce growing exponentially, customers still pay for goods but in a different way, thus adapting the means but not altering the ends of the original system. Instead of interacting with a cashier, a consumer can now purchase most items by interacting with a website on a computer, initiating a transaction that is then processed by people miles away. The overall purpose of the original system within which the cashier existed remains intact, but a new element within the overall world economic system, the Internet, has adapted the means through which that purpose is achieved. The end, however, is still the same: Companies sell products and consumers obtain items they need or desire.

An individual human being exists as a system that has fundamental properties which control and direct its actions and functioning. For example, a human being's body exists as an individual microsystem comprising a massive number of individual elements and systems. Let's name a few of them.

One may consider the skeletal system to be the foundation, existing as a structure which gives rise to the form of the human being. Much like the steel frame body of a car or skyscraper, the skeletal system acts as a container or base for everything else within the human body, helping to keep the body rigid against the force of gravity and serving as an entity which the human form can wrap itself around.

The muscular system serves as a means of movement, like the wheels on a car. The digestive system helps process food and liquids necessary for the functioning of the body, like the engine and fuel tank on a car. The circulatory system moves the fuel and other materials throughout the body to provide the other systems with sustenance. The respiratory system brings oxygen into the body, to be passed along by the circulatory system in order to help the fuel processed in the stomach and intestines to be used. The excretory system eliminates the used fuel like the exhaust pipe on a car, alleviating the harmful byproducts of energy producing reactions. The nervous system controls all the other systems, receiving input from all of them, coordinating them, and assessing the needs of the overall system that is the body. The reproductive system ensures that next year's models will be released, and according to evolutionary theory, they will be more updated versions, slightly better suited for life on this planet at this particular moment in time. However, in both people and cars, there is always the small possibility of defects existing in the next generation.

Without one of these systems, with the exception of the reproductive system, the overall system would not be able to sustain itself. Without the reproductive system, the organism would be unable to pass on its genes—thus, from an evolutionary perspective, failing to fulfill the sole purpose of the organism.

Of course there are many other individual systems making up these larger ones, such as the cells in the body or the DNA within them, but discussions of them are too complex for the purpose of this book. For now, let it be said that nearly every other organism or functioning entity— governments, companies, military forces, economies—requires similar systems, both micro and macro, to function.

Let us examine one seemingly simple system, such as the room that I am currently sitting in. Within this system there are virtually an infinite number of other systems interacting upon and within it. But how does one define this system? By its physical dimensions? By the elements existing within these dimensions at any moment in time? Air, for example, is constantly circulating in and out of the room through the small cracks around the door and window frames. In general, the system itself seems to be intimately connected to what's happening outside of its physical dimensions, with many of the entities and forces existing within or acting upon it at any given moment constantly changing.

There are various categories of entities within this room, but two main ones: the "visibles" and the "invisibles." The visibles would be the physical objects within the room, such as the books on the shelves, the coins scattered across the little table, the calculator next to them, the bed over in one corner of the room, the coat hung on the door, the water that comes out of the faucet, the laptop on this window-sill desk, and myself, to name a few. The invisibles within the room, which are every bit as much a part of the room as are the visibles, would include, the circulating air, gravity forcing everything in the room down toward the ground, time, and all the frequencies of wavelengths from the electromagnetic spectrum, such as radio waves, visible light, and electromagnctic waves.

So after briefly listing just a few of the elements of this seemingly simple system—this 10' x 14' x 18' room—we discover that this simple system is actually quite a bit more complex than it appears. So many elements make up this system, each playing an integral role within it. It is all of these elements that together enable this system to *be* this system. If even one of the invisibles or visibles were removed, the system would be a different system. Imagine if gravity were removed. The system would clearly exist as a different one, with all of the objects floating all over the place.

However, even if something small were removed, such as the one fork in the room, the system would be altered. The absence of the fork changes the system in a way that would affect other entities within the system however slightly. The most obvious entity that would be affected would be me, the human being for which the fork existed in the room in the first place. Picture the adaptations I would have to undergo in order to eat a plate of salad without a fork. There probably would be a much greater mess after I ate anything that necessitates a fork. This, in turn, might cause more water to flow through the system by making after-meal cleanups take longer because of larger messes. It would also block my ability to write during mealtimes, because of the effort and energy involved in trying to avoid contaminating other items in the room with the dressing from the salad. It might also alter my behavior outside the room, thus altering my overall psychology, if I discovered that I liked using a spoon and knife to eat salads and decided to use this technique at the local cafe. However slight this change in behavior, it would still mark my behavior as deviating from the average individual's, and I might come to see myself, therefore, as different, or idiosyncratic.

Another item, the stainless steel cup, exists within its own microsystem—along with the human being, who uses it to wash out his mouth, and the water faucet from which it is filled with water, thereby enabling the human being to make use of it and thus fulfilling its intended purpose. The electrical outlet too, is within its own system, along with all of the electrical appliances within the room, such as the laptop and the cell phone charger. Without one there would be no reason for the other to exist, for the electrical outlet exists so as to provide energy for the electrical appliances, and the appliances might not exist within the room if they couldn't be used within it. Like the electrons and protons within the atom, they exist for each other.

In understanding systems in general, it is helpful, though not always possible, to know their history, and if at all possible their overall conception to death cycle, in order to understand their current state as fully as possible. Hence, in order to understand this system to its utmost, a recounting of the history of each one of the components is needed. For one would hardly be able to understand the person existing as myself if one did not understand my parents and who they are, as well as where they came from and everything else involved in my creation up to this point in time. Now in such investigations, each subsequent level delved into usually decreases the marginal utility, or benefit derived, from further investigations at levels more remote from the subject.

For example, if one wants to understand who I am, the best possible method to acquire the greatest possible quantity of information is to study my physical and mental makeup as a human being. The next best would be to study the contributing factors outside of my physical and mental being, such as my social relations, possessions, as well as the socio-political and economic systems in which I live and have lived in. But such an analysis in the case of this room would be too complex for our current purposes and will be touched upon only later.

To know the room still better, it would be necessary to know the area in which it exists within and plays a role, for the study of microsystems entails the study of macrosystems, and vice versa, if we are to achieve a complete understanding of either one. Even though it may be fairly easy to know something as simple as one of the bananas in the room, to really understand it is a completely different matter. How did the banana get its shape? Why is it yellow? How did this particular banana come to exist within the particular system of this room? What external forces, both natural and human, allowed for the creation of this banana and its transportation to this particular location? Our investigation requires the study of the "larger" forces at play, existing as the macrosystems within which this room resides.

Macrosystems

Macrosystems are the large controlling constituents, where microsystems operate. Macrosystems, like microsystems, are continually at work shaping and controlling everything in the universe—and in many ways they are no different from microsystems. For example, the microsystem existing as a swirl of milk within coffee is in essence not very different from the swirl of air in a large hurricane, or the swirl of planets, stars, and other matter within a spiraling galaxy.

In the human world, as in the rest of the animal kingdom, there exist many "social" macrosystems, such as the economic and political, which play a large *conscious* role in our daily lives. We are, inherently, social animals, and most of our fundamental physiological and psychological needs are met through social systems of our creation and subject to our manipulation. In truth, however, none of these social systems are truly human-created; rather, they are human variations of systems already existing within nature.

Nonsocial systems also play a huge role in our lives, in fact probably a much larger one. However, most nonsocial systems, unlike social ones, we have little to no immediate or direct control over and therefore we most often either forget or adapt to them. These systems are absolutely vital to our existence. Without the Milky Way galaxy (i.e., system), for example, our solar system which is a smaller system within it, would not exist. Each element in the Milky Way, by virtue of its gravitational force, helps keep the Earth within a certain distance from the Sun, making possible temperatures that allow everything that exists on Earth *to* exist. Furthermore, the Earth's rotation around the sun, as mentioned earlier, controls everything by virtue of the changing, cyclical, exposures of sunlight. These

70

forces work invisibly to most humans.

Though it is rarely referred to as such, the nonhuman natural world, like our human one, exists as an economy. The ideas of supply and demand, marginal utility, and comparative advantage were not invented by Adam Smith, but rather were discovered and explained by Smith, enabling humans to manipulate these forces. For these phenomena are key components of every "natural system" existing on this planet. Imagine an ecosystem that consumes more than it can produce: It collapses. The herbivores are running rampant, and are procreating at a rate the carnivores cannot keep up with. They are eating all the plant material in sight, causing a shortage in the supply of plant food, which the plants cannot supply at a fast enough rate to keep that level of consumption going. So the economy crashes, causing the herbivores to starve to death, until equilibrium is reestablished. Now the predators' population has exploded, due to the superabundance of opportunity existing within their market. While their numbers increase at a fast rate, the numbers of herbivores decrease at nearly the same rate, due to increased predation and decreased food supply. This in turn causes the now excessively supplied carnivore market to crash, on account of the declining supply in the now more "expensive" herbivore market.

Evolution in general has been a largely economic system. Look at the vulture who feeds exclusively on carrion in the African Sahara. The system exists in a balance so that every animal has its own particular role to play within it, much like every company plays a role within our economic system or every worker fulfills one within a company. Vultures play the role of a smaller niche company which exists because of the larger company (e. g., lions or hyenas) by taking the excesses that the larger companies cannot sell or use and putting them to their own use. If the larger company existed without this smaller company consuming these excesses, though it undoubtedly would still exist, it would be economically worse off, because of their inability to capitalize on or minimize their excess expenditure. In our example, the lions, also benefit because the vultures both

71

ensure the cleanup of kills that could otherwise spread disease that could harm the lion population as well as helping to fertilize the soil slightly more, as all animals do, through the nutrients contained within their droppings, which then benefit the plants that the new generation of herbivores will feed upon.

Division of labor exists within many colonies of insects, such as ants, bees, and termites. In most species of termites, for example, there exist five different types of termites within the same species. One is the soldier termite, a sterile adult who is considerably larger than the other termites except for the queen. Soldier termites' heads, depending on the species, either have a tube that secretes poison or giant jaws that they use to protect the colony.

Then there are worker termites, male and female sterile adults that are considerably smaller. They collect food, build tunnels, and in general keep the colony functioning. They have developed special "technology" to allow them to digest the wood they eat through a symbiotic relationship with bacteria that live in their gullets.

The nest is tended by another type of worker termite, which works exclusively in the nursery, maintaining the developing pupae within a proper environment. If danger is imminent, as in the case of a flood or an approaching enemy, they move the pupae to a safe location.

The male termite's, only function is to be a lifelong mate with the female. Their entrance into the world is marked by a showy flight from the nest with a female to some distant location, whereupon they shed their wings and mate helping to establish a new colony.

Lastly, the queen, the center of the colony's existence, lives an immobile life, existing as an organism many times larger than all of the other termites. Once she sheds her wings and mates, she establishes a new termite colony and begins her egg-producing life. She can produce eggs for more than ten years, during which she is tended to by the worker termites in the colony.

Political systems are likewise abundant in nature and

assume varying forms. A gorilla group exists as a hierarchy wherein the adult silverback gorilla rules. The adult silverback determines the "laws" of the system as well as enforces them. Under the silverback, there is a stratification of all the females within the group. The highest of the females is the "alpha" female, who is the preferred mate of the silverback. She receives deference from the younger gorillas and teaches them how to raise babies and care for themselves.

Political change within this community can occur abruptly once the silverback has aged. Solitary and small groups of "bachelor" gorillas are a constant threat to silverbacks that already control their own group. Once they feel prepared, these bachelors may try to oust an aging silverback from his position by force, as if in a coup. At the end of this coup, if it is successful, the new ruler will kill all of the babies within the gorilla group so that the females can concentrate on raising his own offspring. This act is much like the cleansing of rival political parties and the destruction of rival parties' symbols after a new government, particularly a totalitarian one, takes over control. These acts are a means of consolidating power for the new ruler by removing any opposition.

In a similar manner to the political change just discussed, though in a completely different realm, chemical reactions replace the current properties of a molecule and establish a whole new set of properties when new elements are introduced. For example, when Sodium (2Na) is added to the aqueous solution of Hydrochloric Acid (2HCl) a dramatic change in properties occur as the atoms of Hydrogen are displaced by the Sodium atoms to form Sodium Chloride, table salt (2NaCl), and Hydrogen gas (H_2). This substitution is possible because Sodium is a more reactive element than Hydrogen which is due to Sodium having a less stable electron arrangement than Hydrogen. Sodium's "political coup or revolution" has completely altered the governing dynamics of the chemicals in this region much like a real political coup or simply a changing of governments does between and within countries.

The entire system of Earth functions as a result of all of

the systems influcncing and constraining it, and as human beings progress in knowledge and technology, a seemingly increasing trend has been to borrow designs already existing within this system for man-made products. This increased technology allows human beings greater flexibility in design, allowing for more complex designs in nature to be emulated.

Airplane design is an example of humans "borrowing" designs that already exist in nature. The long-range B-52 bomber has one of the largest payload capacities as well as one of the largest wingspans in the history of planes. The albatross, a very large seabird which spends much of its life flying above the oceans, has a similar design to that of the B-52. The reason for this similarity is simple; they both are designed to fly within the relatively same system of Earth's atmosphere, and are subject to the same constraints of the laws of aerodynamics. The fact that one is a bird and the other a plane makes little difference as far as the basics of their aeronautical design are concerned. The large wings on both the bird and the plane help to create enough lift to maintain the large amount of weight that they possess, and enable both to stay aloft in the air for as long as possible with a minimum expenditure of energy.

A fighter jet, on the other hand, has the goal of maximizing its speed and maneuverability. The F-14 Tomcat, which has wings that can sweep back into a more condensed position, is a good example. The sweeping back of the wings makes the F-14's front profile smaller, reducing the drag upon its body and thereby making it faster and more maneuverable. This swept-wing design is much like the ones birds of prey have— including the peregrine falcon, the fastest diving bird in the world. The peregrine falcon folds its wings back when diving to catch its prey.

Similarly, the hollow wings used in some aircraft as well as strong new lightweight materials are much like the hollow feathers of birds. The goal of both the human designed and the nature developed wings is to reduce the amount of weight necessary for the respective flying entity to take off while at the same time maintaining the strength necessary not to fall apart under high stress flying conditions. Such human adaptations have increased as the ability to fabricate a wide range of materials has advanced. With the stronger, lighter-weight materials that are increasingly coming into existence in aircraft design, nature will be able to be emulated to a much larger extent.

People have always looked to nature for inspiration since nature has been perfecting its designs for millions of years within the various dynamic systems of the Earth. For instance, Leonardo Da Vinci's flying machine concept arose from his fascination with birds; his notebooks contain extensive notes of the aerodynamics of their flight. If it were not for the birds in the sky, proving the capability for flight within the atmosphere, the very idea of a human being flying might not have even crossed his mind.

However, as humans continue to learn about the systems operating within this world, they will no longer merely seek examples within nature to emulate. With increased knowledge of systems comes an increased capability to adapt, manipulate, and control them—especially as we push beyond Earth's boundaries into space, where there may be no models to inspire us.

Now let us get back to the example of the room that we were looking at earlier. This time we'll look at all of the macrosystems at work within and upon it. To start, let us examine an individual item within the room. We'll then take that knowledge and apply it to outside of the room. In this case, let us examine the box of Multi-Grain Cheerios™ in the glass-covered cupboard. What does it reveal about the larger, outside system in which the room exists?

Let's examine the box first. It is a bright, attention-getting yellow. Highlighted at the bottom are the words "FREE inside: water squirter," with the splashes from the water squirter ad in the picture almost entirely covering the depictions of the actual food inside. As if springing from a pot of gold, four lines, looking much like a rainbow, emanate from the bottom of the package right next to the massive water squirter prize ad. On the lines are four small individual pieces of the actual product— "O's"—with the words "Corn," "Oats," "Rice," and "Wheat" on each line, respectively. In the upper right of the package is a label that says "Complex Carbohydrates" with a check next to it, and of course at the very top is the product's name, "Cheerios™."

Now in examining this package, it is difficult if not impossible to look at it from the perspective of a complete outsider relative to the system it came from, but let's try to dissect it as objectively as possible. Starting with the label "Complex Carbohydrates," we can assume that the outside system is health-conscious, or at least tries to be so. Additionally, there are the references to corn, oats, rice, and wheat, which are all natural "healthful" grains, even though the product itself also contains small amounts of several other ingredients, including tri-sodium phosphate and brown sugar syrup, neither of which are not mentioned on the cover.

Additionally, the four main ingredients mentioned do not originate from the same environment. It could then be concluded that the society involved is based on trade, because the majority of nations do not have sufficiently diverse environments in which all these products.

Next, the main focus of the front cover of the box seems to be on the "FREE water squirter" that is inside every box. This tells us several things. First, such giveaway promotions reveal that most of the population of this society is not worried about obtaining food. Maslow's hierarchy of needs table, which shows the natural progression of human needs, yields support for this idea, because the food is not really highlighted on the cereal box, showing that this society has its physiological need levels fulfilled and is therefore able to concentrate on its psychological needs. Additionally, the packaging itself is quite complex, once again pointing to an advanced industrialized nation. And within this society, children are being catered to as they are bribed with a toy.

Cereal being sold in some poor region in Africa would certainly not advertise a frivolous toy, when many Africans do not have enough food to survive. Indeed, in such an environment, there probably would be no colorful packaging at

76

all, because there would be no need to try to capture consumers' attention when the food itself would be enough to attract the people in such a society.

Consider, too, that the almost complete nonappearance of the actual product on this particular cover indicates that the product itself is probably already known to the consumer who purchases it. The company probably assumes that the consumer knows the product. It may also be partly that the product itself does not have a very flashy appearance that would help sell it. If the product is already known to the consumer, it probably exists as a legally protected brand name controlled by a major corporation within a capitalistic society.

Now imagine all of the various systems that interacted in one way or another to bring this box of cereal into the room. Think of how many steps, each occurring within a network of macro and microsystems that it took for the cereal box to come to exist within this system. Ultimately, my physiological system, formed within the ecological system, impelled its appearance in the room—in that, I am required to eat food in order to procure energy and maintenance materials for my body.

I was driven by a need within my own biological system, existing as my body, to use my metabolic system, composed largely of my cardiovascular system, as fuel in order to walk, using my skeletal and musculature systems along paths created by the political and socioeconomic systems through the use of diverse construction crews, to a chain supermarket built of diverse materials from many regions. I was influenced to shop in this supermarket in large part by my psychological system, which was in turn influenced by my familial system, which believed in the superiority of brand names and chains rather than small markets.

I then walked down the cereal aisle, as cereal for breakfast is part of the cultural system of social norms and habits of which I'm a part, to pick out this box of Cheerios because of my belief in healthy eating which is another sign of the cultural and marketing system in which I grew up. I then walked back down the aisle to the checkout counter to pay for the cereal through the currency (and, thus, the political-economic system) of the area I'm living in; and then walked back down the street to the apartment which I'm renting from a landlord—part of the same socioeconomic system that gave rise to the cereal and the supermarket.

Additionally, how many separate systems were implicated in the box of Cheerios getting to its exact spot in the store where I, as a consumer, could easily find and purchase it? Prior to being placed on the shelf, it sat in a stockroom until the night crew moved it to the shelves, where customers would see it. Prior to the stockroom it was unloaded from a truck filled with other goods. Before it was in the truck it may have been in a loading station and before that in a manufacturing plant, where the packaging and food were combined and sealed. Prior to the manufacturing plant my Cheerios did not exist as they were merely its raw components of corn, oats, rice, wheat, honey, sugar, etc., across several regions of the globe. Before these raw ingredients were shipped to their respective holding areas, they were harvested from the farms in which they grew during a favorable time period that was set by the Earth's rotation around the Sun. Before being harvested, the components were watered on a regular basis via an irrigation system built for the agricultural system by the economic system. Prior to being irrigated, farmers had to plant the seeds which were obtained from previous plants that would become the raw materials used to make Cheerios.

Furthermore, this analysis is leaving out the steps leading to the production of the packaging, which in itself is composed of many raw materials, including the ink that is printed on it. In addition, a professional designer was involved to design the cover. The "FREE water squirter"—its appeal deriving from its association with a recent 3D animated popular culture movie—is made of plastic, and therefore derived from oil. The list goes on and on. Imagine a similar analysis being done with respect to every entity within the room!

Many of the invisible entities within the room are a direct result of some exterior force existing within a larger system. The radio waves have been emitted from radio towers; the electricity, and the electromagnetic radiation emitted from appliances supplied by electricity, created in a local power plant; the water that enters through a long network of pipes has its source in a lake or reservoir. The light that penetrates the windows during the day has its source over 93 million miles away in the fusion reactions of the sun.

Each one of these is connected to its own vast and intricate network of micro and macrosystems. The diverse frequencies of radio waves make use of the electromagnetic spectrum, which also encompasses visible light, and are emitted by oscillating electrons within radio towers that were created by people for the purposes of communication and entertainment. The economic system is, of course, implicated in the radio stations themselves, most of which produce programming in order to make a profit, as well as in the various companies that built the radio stations and the individuals who are paid to talk on the radio. The political system figures in this system, too. In addition to its' intricate connection to the economy, it formulates rules and guidelines for programming and broadcasting in general. The political system is also referenced in much of the content of the news programming on these various stations.

The oscillating electrons within the radio towers constitute another system, with its own history. In order for this technology to exist, it has taken thousands of years for the world's educational systems to produce scientists within the last century able to discover the controlling mechanisms for the emissions of radio waves.

A true in-depth analysis of this room requires several volumes of writing due to the large number of systems that are both within the room and acting upon the room externally. Yet the analysis of this room is no different than an analysis of any other system—for to know any system completely is to know all of the components and the relationships between the components. By knowing all of the components and their relationships, one can know everything.

As the recently developed chaos theory, popularly known

through the so-called butterfly effect, proclaims, "Simplicity resides within complexity." Simply stated, chaos theory contends that all natural processes manifest patterns within them—and that across many disciplines these are the same pattern.

Compare the branching river to the branching of your own blood vessels. One could say that the only major difference is that one carries water and the other blood. Compare the largest branch's pattern with the smallest in the two systems; the intertwining and curving are the same. Examine the difference between a capillary and an artery; the only major difference is that one is larger than the other. Look at the circulation of the Earth's waters and compare it with the circulation of the air; they both follow the same pattern. Compare the penguin with the seagull. One swims, the other flies, but their "machinery" is similar, with each being built to survive within a different arena. Look at the social patterns and organizations of ants vis-à-vis those of people.

Have you ever noticed the way a cigarette's smoke rises gently in a straight line and then shortly thereafter breaks down into chaos? Mathematical investigations have yielded an equation that yields both the pattern exhibited by rising cigarette smoke and the shapes of leaves and branches. We are all part of one System, operating according to the same basic principles.

Putting It All Together

"The System" is the system in which we live. In its entirety it is an unknowable element, but through its component parts its patterns can be perceived, known, and controlled—and applied elsewhere.

The System is unknowable because it is vast and intricate. It is as if one were to take a swim in the ocean and say that they have swum the entire body of water. No one really knows how far the System extends. Modern physicists try to predict such matters, but the infinitude of things cannot be known from one small speck of a planet amidst an entire cosmos so vast as to take us many, many lifetimes to travel. We are only looking from one point within an immense universe. But hope exists in knowing the System, for just as one may know oneself though hardly understanding all of the processes continually undergoing flux within, the System can be known in much the same way though more complex.

It has been said in this book that knowing yourself is the most important thing one can do if you seek to understand everything. Though there are many reasons for the importance of knowing yourself, perhaps one of the major ones is that doing so enables us to know one element of this world, of this System, so intimately as to wake up everyday and experience its existence as part and parcel of, and existing within, this System. Thereby, an understanding of the System is capable through the patterns of one's own existence. To understand it as you understand yourself.

IV.

Duality...
the ends of the
spectrum.

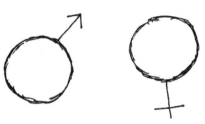

"Knowledge has two extremes."

- Blaise Pascal

DUALITY is a concept that most people have been familiar with since kindergarten. Of course the concept was not stated as duality, but rather as *opposites*: hot-cold, happy-sad, day-night, black-white, rich-poor.

Most children learning about opposites probably did not realize that they were learning anything special. But they were. The concept of duality is a radical one that lays the foundation for the System and all systems within it. Systems exist within a constant state of flux. Flux is possible only when there are two poles to oscillate between. Every known entity within this dichotomous System lies along a conceptual continuum between two extremes. Some of these spectrums are longer than others, such as in good and bad, while others are shorter comprised of in the most extreme case, just two points, such as binary.

Some may try to refute the concept of a dichotomous state within which the System exists by adducing, for example, the various states of the molecule H_2O, which can exist as a solid, a liquid, or a gas. However, these merely represent different excitation states, or energy levels, of the constituent molecules, with the solid being the least and the gas being the most excited.

Dualities are the fundamental component of the next chapter's topic, cycles, which are fluctuations that exist between polar extremes. In addition, the mind, divisions and classifications, and systems are all intricately implicated in the web knitted by the dualities of the world. In all systems, disciplines, and concepts, a dichotomy of components or ideas are present. Understanding this element, from which the foundation of the world is built, is vital to understanding everything. Likewise, in the story of Genesis in the Old Testament, dualities are represented as being foundational to the composition of the Earth. God creates the heavens and the earth, light and darkness, morning and evening, male and female. In this system, one pole gives rise to the other pole, for what is hot if there is no cold?

Dualities Everywhere

Dualities are present everywhere one looks, because dualities are intricately connected to systems. Some dualities exist within finite spectrums with little ambiguity, whereas others, being subjective, exist with much ambiguity, never being able to reach either pole definitively.

To take one of the most finite dualities, binary computer language consists of nothing more than 0's and 1's. Although not opposites in the sense that hot and cold are, the 0's and 1's work like opposites in allowing for the transmission of data through alternations between them. In a sense, binary computer language exists as a "perfect" duality, for there exists no spectrum and therefore no ambiguities between the two numbers. Everything is either one or the other.

Another simple human-created duality that is a little more ambiguous than binary computer language is the traffic light, which allows for three settings: green = go, yellow = prepare to stop and red = stop. It creates a system that is seemingly near perfect, with two members representing extremes and the other an in-between position. However, this system allows for ambiguity, as do almost all other human systems, because the yellow is not a definite stop or go. It could be either, and is therefore open to interpretation. One individual might see a yellow light and stop, while another continues driving.

Ultimately, the ambiguity in this system is due to the room left within the system for peoples' subjective judgment regarding what the appropriate decision is in a situation, whether it involves a moral choice or any particular action. In human affairs there never really are any clear-cut cases wherein one can generalize and be correct 100 percent of the time, because of the differences existing between peoples' personalities, experiences, and beliefs. The major problem all of the psychological disciplines continue to face is the considerable number of exceptions to almost every psychological principle. These exceptions leave a highly complex spectrum between an infinite number of poles to examine.

Take, for example, the situation with respect to morality and personality attributes. As Aristotle discusses in his *Nicomedian Ethics*, no one person is the epitome of courage, kindness, and other moral attributes. Each person has within them the capability to exemplify each one of these qualities, but only to a certain extent. To say that one has exhibited ultimate courage, for example, is to say that one has faced the ultimate fear-inducing situation. Such a situation, however, can hardly be said to exist, for no matter how fearful one thinks a situation is there is almost always the possibility for there to be a more fearful one. For example, a person who watches a drive-by shooting take place arguably does not experience the same degree of fear as a prisoner would during the reigns of terror of the Khmer Rouge in Cambodia or the Nazis in Germany.

What is a good individual? Most would likely consider an individual who commits more good acts than bad acts to be good. So let us consider an individual who has lived a seemingly saintly life doing nothing but good acts for others, but in their heart they have done good only for the benefit of feeling good (i.e., about doing good) themselves. Should he or she still be regarded as a good person, though (s)he only acted selfishly, or does (s)he move farther along the continuum away from ultimate good, closer to the ultimate bad pole?

As we stated earlier, definitions of human psychological states are difficult, because unlike in the physical sciences, where measurements can be taken, there are no methods, as of this writing, to definitively measure the human mental condition. In general, that is as of now a highly subjective task, requiring the individual to verbally report his or her condition or for someone to observe them. Though some brain imagery technology exists, it is still very primitive.

If researchers could view the physical brain in action in real-life situations, it might be possible to conclude that a certain pattern of resonation, "X," among brain cells corresponds to the general state "Y" in the brain. But differences abound even among the resonations viewed, for the human mind is a variable that is considerably more difficult to control than, for example, the climate within a testing room, and every person's brain is structured and operates differently.

Now, imagine that the seemingly saintly individual, who this time does good acts for unselfish purposes, one day, commits murder. Surely he must be judged to have been a good person for having lived a saintly life, with the intention of helping others, for many years; but does this single incident of murder define an individual who now must be considered to belong closer to the completely bad pole? Such an ambiguity exists because of our lack of information as to why the person committed murder.

Ambiguities in morality are one of the major problems with the legal systems of the world. Laws are written so as to punish the perpetrator of a crime to the extent that he or she broke the law. But can any law truly serve the cause of pure justice? Each case is, or has the potential to be, different. Imagine an individual who kills someone who murdered their beloved spouse ten years before. Could not the victim's spouse be said to have sought "justice" by committing this particular murder? Or, at least, can the individual be entirely faulted?

What about the judge and jury? The determination of a person's "guilt" or "innocence" rests on subjective judgments.

86

Because of the ambiguities between different situations and the fact that humans are determining the person's fate, laws must be adapted to allow the punishment to fit the crime, by allowing for a range of punishments for any given crime. But this is difficult when there is no black and white, only gray.

Take any of the human psychological conditions, and one will discover that they all fall in between an infinite number of poles. Contrast psychological conditions to *physiological* states existing within people, such as, life and death. These have relatively known start and end dates, though as we see in debates about abortion, or about prolonging or withholding life support, controversy in this regard exists as well; for how does one truly define the onset of life—or, in ambiguous circumstances, its termination?

Almost all things that can be measured with any degree of accuracy have extremes that exist as knowns. For example, heat is a reflection of the excitation states of atoms as a result of varying energy levels. Therefore, the more excited the atom, the higher the temperature. This duality is clear-cut, because objective instruments exist that can measure the precise excitation states of different atoms. Hence, the continuum of temperature is concrete, especially by comparison with more subjective human systems. There even exists an absolute zero, 0 degrees Kelvin, which corresponds to a complete lack of energy within atoms—although this state is believed to exist only within the environment of a laboratory.

The electrical forces which hold the various elements of atoms together likewise exist along a continuum, with the positive extreme at one end and the negative at the other. The opposing electrical charges that emanate from protons and electrons create the duality that is necessary for the atom to exist. To the extent that protons and electrons balance each other out as well as how much of the outer electron shell is filled is the degree in which the atom is stable.

The electromagnetic spectrum exists as a polarity as well, with radio waves, with the longest wavelengths, at one end of the spectrum, and x-rays, with the shortest wavelengths, at the other end. In between, many other waves exist with other properties, including visible light. In actuality, all the points along this spectrum exist only as waves: not as x-rays, light, or radio broadcasts, but just as waves. It was human beings who delineated the points along this spectrum through the use of names.

Before we continue describing some of the numerous dualities that exist, take a look at the table at the end of the chapter for a more comprehensive list of dualities within the world. It is important to be able to recognize the various dichotomies that exist, for everything exists in a dichotomy.

Likes Conglomerate . . . Poles Conglomerate

The ancients thought the world consisted of four basic elements: Earth, Water, Air, and Fire. In their belief system, each element existed as a layer of the world, with Earth being the element most closely drawn downward, followed by Water, Air, and lastly, Fire. Each element, they believed, sought to return to the layer to which it belonged. This explained why objects fell, why lakes and oceans existed on top of land, why Fire would always rise, and the like.

Today we know that the world is composed of many more elements, and that these so-called layers exist because of gravity acting upon the inherent masses of different elements, giving some a greater density, while others less. The primary concept remains. Lakes exist because water accumulates at the lowest points on the Earth—because it does not have the solidity of dirt or rock, so that it could come to rest high up on a hillside without either slowly trickling downward or evaporating back up into the sky, only to fall down again, as rain, in some other place. It is always seeking the lowest point on the Earth.

Sometimes likes exist together because they were created in or adapted to the same environment. For example, gold and silver are not found scattered around a country in near equal proportions, but rather are found in large concentrations in particular areas due environmental conditions that cause both to come into existence.

Likewise, people born in a small town or large city are likely to stay in or want to return to a small town or large city, respectively, because that is where they grew up and subsequently were formed with their own unique characteristics. Thus, the city dweller is most likely going to stay in the city, because that is the lifestyle that he or she has grown accustomed to—and in general, people do not change unless acted upon forcefully by some exterior entity. For example a person who escaped death from one of the World Trade Center towers during the attacks on 9/11 would stand a very good chance of being fundamentally changed forever.

Both small town folk and city dwellers are therefore likely to congregate with like individuals, because that is what they are accustomed to and feel comfortable with. However, at heart, both have the same fundamental desires and fears, both fundamentally wanting life and happiness, while fearing death and misery. How they both maintain life while avoiding death are the same, but how they attain or ward away happiness and misery respectively are different due to their individual preferences and adaptations developed through their environment.

Aside from regional differences between people, ideology, age, ethnicity, nationality, and a host of other differences separate people into their respective poles. Part of the reason why people stay with their own is that it provides comfort to them because they are validated by being around others with similar interests and beliefs.

The result of such tendencies is that the microsystems that like-minded people create exist in relatively stable forms in the short term but are nevertheless, continuously undergoing flux in the long term. The overall system may become more *un*stable, however, because of the various microsystems, composed of different sets of like-minded people, coming into conflict. These confrontations are due to different conglomerations not mixing on a regular basis. This is not to say that they do not mix in terms of, for example, riding on the same subways and buses, but in meaningful ways such as hanging out so that each others' humanness can be discovered and appreciated. Without meaningful ways of mixing, the results can be destructive as their fear and distrust of each other becomes inflamed from their mutual ignorance. When a base is suddenly put with an acid, there is little time for each to adapt to each other's chemical makeup.

Tour a large city and one can see likes conglomerating as a regular feature of the environment. Take San Francisco or New York, for example. Each city has its own areas where particular immigrants have settled, such as Chinatown or Little Italy. Banding together enables immigrants, who have traditionally faced discrimination from the natives of a country, to acquire a certain level of power and security. They live with each other and look out for each other because of their similar traditions, culture, language, and overall situation in a foreign land.

In nature, animals have a tendency to congregate with others like themselves, too. Many prey animals, for example, tend to congregate in large groups so as to provide themselves with a certain degree of safety from predators. For fish, these groups are called schools, while for hoofed mammals, herds, and for birds, flocks, to name a few.

Moreover, reptiles have a tendency to exist in greater proportion in comparison to other topographical regions vis-à-vis mammals in areas characterized by high temperature and low precipitation. However, mammals will exist in a greater proportion with respect to reptiles in regions characterized by cool weather and high precipitation. They both "choose", or more appropriately, have adapted to their regions by developing their respective and unique properties, which allow one to exist with little water, needing external heat to heat its own body, whereas the other has the capability to survive cold weather with its own built-in heating system but needs relatively copious quantities of water to function. Both exist where they exist out of necessity, due to the way each was created. If for example, a species of snake that is endemic to a desert region is suddenly placed in the artic, the snake is not going to fare well. The same, though for different reasons, could be said about a human being from Nepal who only speaks Nepali being suddenly dropped into a small town in the Mid-west of the United States.

People have often referred to rain forests as ecological "cities," because a wide range of different types of animals, can live and thrive in a high-heat, high-precipitation environment serving many organisms' needs.

Energy levels tend to conglomerate as well. A high-energy negatively charged entity will attract a high-energy positively charged one much more than it will attract a low-energy positively charged one. High-energy entities attract one another in order to balance each others' charges out to a more neutral level.

Walking through a city, an individual who at that moment has a high energy level will likely be drawn to an environment that reflects his or her current state, if that state is being enjoyed. Conversely, individuals with low energy levels will likely be repelled by high-energy-level environments and will instead seek quiet, restful environments that reflect their current mood unless they seek to change their current energy level. Different people have different overall energy levels, which almost always control such decisions.

Polar Extremes Interact

There is an old saying that says that "opposites attract." In many cases this is true, because polar extremes have a moderating effect upon one another. Hot and cold water placed together results in warm water or a balance between the two. The overall System continually seeks stability, or equilibrium through the juxtaposition of polarities.

Now this principle, of polar extremes interacting, may seem surprising, given our previous discussion regarding the tendency of similar entities to conglomerate. The fact of the matter, though, is that two opposite poles along the same respective continuum in any system are attracted to one another to one degree or another, and for better or for worse. These attractions are a result of the instability of polar extremes. It is difficult to sustain a polar extreme for a long period of time, for the System continually seeks equilibrium. Polar extremes therefore are capable of inducing tremendous amounts of change within a system due to their volatility.

For example, when an atom is lacking a stable outer shell of electrons, there is the possibility that another atom will come along, forming a molecule with the first atom, thereby making it more stable—for atoms tend to try to fill their entire outer shell so as to attain the most stable possible configuration. Ions of elements also tend to try to find an extra electron or lose one in order to balance out the inner and outer electrical charges.

The sexes represent an obvious duality. Without the female sex, males would not exist, and without the male sex, females would not exist. The one brings forth the other. Excess testosterone as well as overall societal influences, lead males toward a more aggressive existence, whereas in females, estrogen as well as overall societal influences tend toward a more passive existence. Other characteristics differ between the sexes as well. When a person is part of a couple, the "couple" is a moderating force in the lives of both parties, balancing out their extremes, which would otherwise tend to yield states of greater instability for each. Even the sexual organs exist as opposites, with one existing as a void and the other as an existent, the one completing the other and vice versa.

Sometimes the reactions that occur when two polar extremes are placed together are explosive, due to the strong characteristics that each has in their own pole. When an acid is mixed with a base, a strong chemical reaction occurs, often an explosion. A highly negatively charged item in close proximity to a highly positively charged item will create a spark composed of an excess of electrons that jump from the negative item to the positive one. If a feminist with a "male chauvinist" are in the same room, an explosive reaction may occur. Similarly, "explosions" may occur when an environmentalist and a strip miner or an atheist with a devout Christian are together..

Reality TV shows are an example of "polar opposites"

being put in close proximity to one another. Producers will place vastly different people together precisely to ensure that they have an explosive combination, and hence a show with tension and instability. These characteristics are more stimulating to the general television audience than a show characterized by calm and stability. Explosions of one kind or another often occur when two opposites are thrown together, for the poles have strong properties that are predominantly unstable and opposing. If the poles are not obliterated during their encounter, then the interaction between the two often yields moderate entities.

In human beings, the presentation of two contrasting entities deceives our sensory systems. Let us call the principle that explains this fact, the contrast principle. Since this principle can be used to deceive the human brain, it is an effective tool in marketing. Advertisers, like predatory organisms, try to coax their prey into traps, so that they can make money by selling their product to those who fall for their marketing schemes. For example, today, in the midst of winter, I took the London subway, or "Underground," and saw many ads portraying the opposite climate from the one that the city was at the time undergoing. One ad, a giant tourism ad encouraging travel to Turkey, had the words "Experience the warmth of this sun-baked land," with a landscape of nothing but the purest blue waters and sky, a palm tree, and a scantily clad tanned woman who looked as if she had just starred in the attack of the fifty-foot woman as her image took up nearly a third of the total ad space.

Now, London in the midst of winter is not the sunniest or warmest of locations, not to mention the fact that the only bikini-clad women within sight are those at the local "gentlemen's club." Therefore, this ad plays upon the contrast principle quite well by offering people the promise of experiencing the exact opposite of the traditionally gloomy weather in London. Words like "warm" and "sun" favorably contrast with the more commonly spoken words "dreary" and "cold." The advertisers specifically chose elements in their billboard that would contrast favorably with London invoking the average Londoner to have a greater than normal appreciation for the sun and warmth of

Turkey rather than another country.

Films are another medium that make use of the contrast principle extensively. Have you ever noticed the way a commercially viable film will tend to continually go from extreme action to little action and back? This is the contrast principle at work. Imagine a movie with only action. It may have the same effect as living near train tracks, where one initially notices the trains going by but after a while becomes used to them. Likewise, one becomes desensitized to the loud noises and fast-moving pictures in the movie and the film therefore becomes somewhat boring, losing its original impact. Therefore filmmakers vary a film in all of its aspects—sound and pacing as well as images—always invoking the necessary contrast in order to maintain excitement and interest throughout the movie.

The whole basis of most jokes and of much comedy in general, is also based upon the contrast principle. As Freud put it, "the effect of a joke comes about through bewilderment being succeeded by illumination." He defines joking as "the ability to find similarity between dissimilar things—that is, hidden similarities." Isaac Asimov says humor results from a sudden, unexpected alteration in point of view. Another way the contrast principle can create humor are the clichéd comedy teams that consist of the straitlaced individual and the goofball. Examples of these teams are Laurel & Hardy, Abbott & Costello, Kramden & Norton ("The Honeymooners"), and Penn & Teller. Laurel & Hardy for example, in addition to their personality contrasts, have very visible, exaggerated physical contrasts as well with Laurel being the shorter skinny guy and Hardy being the taller fat guy. If both members of the comedy team were goofballs, there would not be any contrast for them to play off of and therefore, humor is unlikely to result. In a way, the goofball without a contrasting element (i.e., the straight man) would become normal to the audience within their particular system.

Place your hand into a bucket of freezing water and then, shortly thereafter, into a bucket of warm water. The warm water will seem to be hot. Try this in the other direction by sticking your hand first in hot water and then warm and the warm water will then seem cold. This too is the contrast principle at work in your brain's cognitive system, interpreting contrasting perceptual signals.

The reason this works is that everything is relative. You see a man driving a BMW sports car and you may think that the man is rich. However, if you see that same man driving next to someone driving a brand-new Rolls Royce, suddenly the BMW driver does not seem all that rich anymore, even though both cars are in the upper echelon of automobiles. See a man rob an old lady, and you may think that he is an evil man. If you subsequently see a man ruthlessly kill this old lady, however—and two others who get in the way—the man who only *robbed* the old lady now seems not so bad.

When one experiences one polar extreme, any other stimulus that is more moderate along the same spectrum will seem to be closer to the opposite extreme than it is, even though it may actually reside somewhere near the middle. Knowing dichotomies is what allows one to perceive, understand, and be aware of this phenomenon, using the contrast principle.

As one final example, recently my mother discovered the value of this principle when she was pulled over by a policeman. Just after pulling her over and before writing her a ticket, he stopped another car that had rolled through the same stop sign. This other car's driver became irate at the officer, tearing up the ticket and throwing it on the ground. When the officer, who was prepared to write my mother a ticket, came back to her, who during the whole incident remained very calm and polite, she was let go with only a warning, for she must have seemed like an angel by comparison with the other, hysterical driver.

Putting It All Together

Dichotomies are known to most of us since we were children. Each pole within a dichotomy exists not in and of itself, but only as the opposite of the other pole within its particular continuum. Without the existence of light there could be no dark.

Entities within dichotomies tend to exist in equilibrium. Extremes within the System are relatively rare by comparison with moderates due to their instability and reactivity. In trying to reach this equilibrium, extremes often will give rise to their exact opposite. Fascism arose during roughly the same era as communism, and both now are nearly non-existent with more moderate democracies becoming the equilibrium.

An important realization is that extremes—existing in the form of advantages and disadvantages, strengths and weaknesses—exist within each other. An item's strength is also its weakness; its weakness is also its strength. One does not exist without the other.

If for example, an individual's strength lies in their physical attractiveness, then their attractiveness is also where their weakness lies. An individual who is physically beautiful usually, and especially in the absence of a moderating parental force, tends not to develop other aspects of themselves, such as their minds. Their social needs are usually met on account of their physical attractiveness, and the need to develop themselves into a well-rounded and complete individual is not present to the extent that it might be in the case of a less physically appealing individual. They can perhaps enter the entertainment industry or marry wealth on the strength of their looks alone, or advance through the work world by using their looks to manipulate others.

To understand dichotomies to the fullest, one must understand cycles. The next chapter will present such information and will therefore yield a more in-depth analysis of dichotomies.

jealousy	arrogance		positve	negative
hatred	love		up	down
enemy	ally		hot	cold
stingy	generous		strong	weak
apathy	empathy		big	small
cowardice	foolhardy		loud	soft
poor	rich		right	left
evil	good		free	imprison
carefree	serious		slow	fast
mean	kind		alkaline	base
ignorant	knowledgable		stable	unstable
death	birth		dark	light
liberal	conservative		clean	dirty
chaos	order		transparent	opaque
discord	harmony		spicy	bland
blind	seeing		go	stop
non-being	being		harmony	discord
decline	advance		harmless	dangerous
destroy	build		happy	sad
war	peace		calm	stress

V.

Cycles...
flux between poles.

> *"All things have their ends and cycles. And when they have reached*
> *their highest point, they are in their lowest ruin, for they cannot last*
> *for long in such a state. Such is the end for those who cannot moderate*
> *their fortune and prosperity with reason and temperance."*

> *- François Rabelais*

CYCLES exist as the fluctuations between dualities. Accordingly, the last chapter and this one are intricately linked. For as we briefly explained, one polar extreme tends toward the other polar extreme. In a fluctuating system, no lasting balance will ever be reached, only an ongoing *un*-balance. Therefore, knowledge of the cycles that occur between poles becomes exceptionally important if we want to understand all things.

Cycles exist within every system—from something as ingrained in our minds as the 24-hour night-and-day cycle, created by the Earth's rotation, to something a little more obscure like the hydrologic cycle, which yields the interplay between rainfall and evaporation; From one of the briefest cycles, involving an electron's orbit around its nucleus, which takes a fraction of a second, to one of the longest possible cycles, existing in theoretical form and without scientific opposition as the universe's expansion and contraction.

The well-known quotation from Ecclesiastes, familiar from the Pete Seeger melody and, especially, the recording by the folk-rock group the Byrds, expresses the inherent necessity of cycles in the scheme of life:

> *To everything there is a season*
> *And a time for every purpose under heaven:*
> *A time to be born, and a time to die;*
> *A time to plant, and a time to reap;*
> *A time to kill, and a time to heal;*
> *A time to weep, and a time to laugh . . .*

The System is set up so that everything naturally has a "season." One's mind and overall being, for example, could not function or survive in a world where they need to integrate into so many different systems, if they only existed within an emotional space of anger, elation, or misery all the time. But each one of these emotional states does exist within every living individual—as and in the course of a "season." Some just live in one or another of these poles for longer "seasons" than others. On a physical level, how could the body exist if it underwent only anabolic or catabolic reactions? The body needs both processes in order to operate effectively. Everything tries to return to stasis—to stability.

As we discussed earlier, people have many cycles, including but not limited to the hormonal cycles. Without an understanding of the cycles within oneself, one will be caught unawares with respect to their past, present, and future states. Appreciating one's cycles as a reflection of, and in relation to, many external cycles gives one a sense of the true nature of reality.

Cycles, as with everything else, exist within two human time-referenced categories: microcycles and macrocycles. However, a more meaningful distinction may be that between "regular" and "irregular" cycles. Some cycles are regular, like the Earth's orbit around the Sun which occurs during a time frame that is roughly 365.25 Earth days. Other cycles, however, are more *ir*-regular, involving many more fluctuating factors than just the period of rotation around the Sun. These cycles can seem to occur at seemingly random time periods, like those based on the calculations, speculations, and hopes of the human mind. The business cycle is an example of a cycle based partly on the outlook of humans.

Regular & Irregular

Regular cycles are those that seem to best fit under the category of the mathematical sciences, such as physics and computer science. Regular cycles exist as definite or near-definite patterns that can be predicted with a good probability of accuracy.

As we mentioned before, the system comprising the Earth and the Sun, wherein the Earth's rotation around the Sun exists as a cycle, in turn creates an abundance of other cycles on the Earth, that are dependent upon the varying angles and distances between the two celestial bodies. We experience this system's cycles as *seasons*. The seasons dictate many things on the surface of the planet, such as the annual breeding seasons for many animals or the increased precipitation that the "rainy season" brings in different parts of the world.

The seasons are such a large factor on this planet that various items within the System are sometimes metaphorically referred to as experiencing their spring, summer, fall, or winter. A business struggling during a downturn in the economy may be in its "winter" months, going dormant trying to survive a drought within the economic system and hoping for rain so as to be able to see "spring." A persons lifetime can be described by the seasons as hc or she experiences "spring" as he or she grows and develops, "blossoming" to become a full-fledged adult in the peak months of summer, retiring in late fall, and living the remaining days basking in summer memories while living more sedentary lives, until the end of their winter months.

However, throughout ones life, one may experience *many* springs, summers, falls, and winters, because although life exists as one long cycle, there are an infinite number of smaller cycles within it and along different spectrums. For example, temperatures rise and fall on a daily basis due to the night-and-day cycle, but have their yearly continuum of temperature fluctuation as well, because of the various distances and angles by which the Earth is aligned vis-à-vis the Sun throughout the year.

As with temperatures, almost all things have a cycle based on the changing amount of sunlight throughout the year. Plants only begin to flower, after a period of reduced sun exposure followed by increased sun exposure, when their particular location on Earth is exposed to longer days of sunlight during spring. Some annual flowers will then become pollinated, producing seeds to help create next years flowers, dying before the year's end. Deciduous trees after being barren of leaves during the winter will begin to acquire foliage during this time to make use of the increased sunlight, a necessary component of photosynthesis, which is the process in which plants create their own food. As the days grow shorter and the sunlight less intense, these species of trees in more northern climates, but often not in southern ones, will shed their leaves taking back some of the food in the leaves in preparation for dormancy in the winter. These leaves, in business terms, were laid off, as company sales declined before winter.

The seasons differ according to the longitude of a location on Earth. As stated before, everything exists within a system that has a dichotomous spectrum. Locations on Earth are no different. The two poles on Earth exist as the extremes experiencing the longest and shortest days on Earth, but always experiencing the coldest weather because of their angles vis-à-vis the Sun. When one is experiencing 19 hours of daylight, the other is experiencing 19 hours of darkness.

The human-invented convention of time also has definite cycles, largely because people created it for that purpose. As a visual aid in imagining time as a cycle, imagine a clock with a swinging pendulum, where every swing represents one second. Similar to the human invention of computer binary language with its two poles, time has its own finite cycles with days and years, being defined with respect to the Earth's rotation, around its axis and its revolution around the Sun. In respect to these natural cycles, people have incrementally divided up these larger natural cycles into more arbitrary artificial ones of months (variable unit), weeks, hours, minutes, seconds, milliseconds and so forth. People also created the artificial units of eons, millennia, centuries, decades, months, and weeks to help reference more macro level time references. These units of time are used to measure the cycles of other systems, however, they are all relative and arbitrary.

Politically, many countries and organizations have a set number of years between elections. Seasons exist within this cycle more subtlety and irregularly. For example, when a leader of a country is first elected, the leader has to become accustomed to the way that his or her complex system of government works. The new leader is in this sense similar to a little child, learning how things operate. Gradually, after some time has passed, the leader has a better sense of how to accomplish things. He or she may become more confident or even arrogant, like a teenager who awakens to a newly found perspective and thinks they can now function as an adult.

As elections start to draw near, still more changes become apparent. The true individual inside the leader often becomes dormant, as the politician inside the leader plays into the populace's desires and expectations in order to get reelected. The leader therefore may become something of a pseudo-self until he or she is reelected, whereupon, at least in countries with a two-term limit such as the United States, they can reemerge to return to their true self, this time without concern over being reelected.

However, as with all things, a leader's tenure must end, so leaders experience a winter in which they begin to reflect upon their term of service, much like a dying individual reflecting on his or her life. They think about how they will be remembered. Sometimes, as if finalizing a will, they may use their waning power, their last opportunity for action, to push through items that may not necessarily be popular but that they desire or believe morally necessary or otherwise essential to the nation's welfare. Of course this is a general discussion, for each country has a unique government, each leader has a unique mind with its own systems and purposes, and there are many micro and macro cycles—i.e., current events—to attend to within this dynamic system.

Economically, businesses exist within similar cycles, but with respect to their shareholders instead of their voters; thus, companies have to provide quarterly reports stating their earnings or losses and their plans for the future. Many "votes" are often lost after a company reports lower than expected earnings.

Extremes Swing to Extremes

There is a very simple principle: the closer a dualistic system nears one polarity, the more likely it is to swing toward the other polarity, as close to the new one as it was to the other. The basis for this principle is Newton's laws of motion. Newton's first law states that:

An object at rest will tend to stay
at rest unless it is acted upon.
An object in motion will stay in
motion unless acted upon.

So if something has been in one state for a period of time, it will continue to stay in that state unless is it propelled to do otherwise. This is the concept of inertia.

A direct example of this law is that of a ball rolling down a ramp that is curved on both sides. When the ball is released at the top of one side, the ball, disregarding friction, rolls to the same height on the opposite side. If the ball is released midway down, the ball will roll midway up on the other side. The addition of friction will cause the ball to slow, and it will finally find its resting place in the middle. It is on the basis of this fundamental example that we can begin our analysis of extremes cycling to extremes.

People and many other things are the same way. A person who has had a certain personality or body or lifestyle tends to stay that way unless acted upon by an external force, such as the death of someone else, becoming famous, or getting cancer. A carefree personality, likewise, will tend to remain carefree unless acted upon. Sometimes the only force that needs to act upon such an individual is age, as they find themselves no longer youthful-looking, which may force them to adapt, and in so doing they may become a little more serious.

Newton's second law states:

The rate of change of momentum of a body is equal to the resultant force acting on the body and is in the same direction.

Quite simply, this law deals with forces acting upon objects. However, this law like the last provides insight into a whole array of other realms that it was originally not meant to describe.

Established economies, for example, tend toward gradual change due to an infinite number of forces acting upon them. Changing culture, governmental policies, natural conditions, productivity, and a country's overall role and image in the world, to name a few, all have major influence over the economy. Each one exerts a force that either directs the economy up or down and to a degree that is equal to its extremity in comparison to the existing system. The force applied can not be given a definite number due to its complexity, unlike the force generated when a person pushes a cart, but nevertheless a force still exists even though we do not at this time have any finite means to measure it.

The force applied to an economy when supply shortages

of oil increase the cost of gasoline is determinant upon the extent that the price is changed and that the oil is necessary to the economy. Extreme spikes in the cost of oil in economies that depend upon it for energy can be devastating. People will suddenly have less money to spend elsewhere, causing companies that do not make their money from oil to lose money and be forced to cut costs including letting go of their workers so that they can stay in business.

In the vast majority of cases, extreme spikes are not sustainable in the long run. In this case, due to the high cost of oil, suppliers will be tempted to sell more oil or to work on producing more oil so that they can capitalize on the rising prices. This increase in the supply will drive prices down. The problem with this example though is that if the demand is undergoing sustained growth, the natural counterbalancing act of supply-demand is unable to function. Worse yet, the Earth's supply of oil is decreasing causing an extremely out of balanced system.

Forces are at work to balance this system through the acquisition and discovery of new oil sources, changing public perceptions, and the encouragement of mass transit alternatives. Additionally, the development of natural renewable energy sources is drawing demand away from oil, slightly at the current moment, but will eventually replace oil in the overall energy systems of the world. Currently, though all such efforts are dwarfed by the gigantic demand for oil.

In other systems such as the supply and demand of the hottest new children's toy before Christmas, demand is exceptionally high. The supply can not keep up or is purposely kept down to maintain demand. Often after Christmas, the same toys that had a huge demand and limited supply will oscillate to the other extreme as the toy becomes over-produced to try to meet demand. This over-production prompts after Christmas sales to try to once again increase demand with lower prices. The system continuously tries to reach equilibrium where supply and demand are equal.

Newton's laws of motion are so pervasive that the reaction two people may have with regards to finding a dollar bill can be explained with his laws. The first person, person X, suddenly discovers a dollar bill on the ground hidden among some shrubs. The force such an event will have upon person X depends upon person X's "economic mass". If person X is a millionaire, his economic mass is large and consequently, the force as determined by the equation, "F = m * a", is small in comparison to his economic mass. However, to person Y who is a homeless person with just twenty dollars in their pocket. The mass in the force equation is the quantity of money which is in this case one dollar. The acceleration can be considered to be the sudden discovery of the money in that precise moment. The force upon person Y is comparatively large.

Now, imagine a person who for all practical purposes is at rest in terms of personality and overall lifestyle. Suddenly, the same person decides to start exercising and embarks upon a daily morning jog. This newly initiated daily jog if maintained will act as a force of change upon the person and act to "move" them in a new direction at a momentum that is determined based upon the determination the person has to succeed and their physical and mental mass prior to the new running regime. The person may start enjoying the new feeling of health and start eating healthier and become interested in other ways of being healthy. Additionally, the person will be more relaxed and happier due to chemical changes within the mind from exercising which in turn will have resultant forces upon the environment such as making those around them happier or more inspired

Newton's third law deals with the dual nature of reality and how each force that is applied in the world results in an exactly opposite force of the same magnitude. To take a brief example, imagine a person decides to donate a twenty dollar bill to a charity. The resultant forces that arise are two: the donator is twenty dollars poorer and the charity is twenty dollars richer. As Newton's third law states:

All forces occur in pairs, and these two forces
are equal in magnitude and opposite in direction.

To stretch our understanding of cycles and illustrate Newton's third law a little better, let us pose a question that may be considered rather controversial, though good for our purposes precisely because it is extreme. Did Adolph Hitler's life or Jesus of Nazareth's life result in more good for the world? Now, obviously, most intelligent, decent individuals would without a doubt say Jesus has done more good for the world, because according to the Bible, he preached about the importance of love and compassion toward all of one's fellow human beings.

Hitler, on the other hand, was a major cause of the worst war that mankind was ever engaged in. He killed millions of unarmed Jews in addition to millions of other civilians. Even the thought of Hitler being considered as even remotely good would be revolting to many, and quite understandably. But if one views one as entirely good and the other as entirely evil, this would be missing an important aspect of their lives: the influence that their respective lives had upon the Earth after their deaths. The force that each one of their lives had was met with an equal but opposite force during and subsequently after their lives.

Hitler, as a direct result of his actions before and during the Second World War, gave rise to a whole new perspective with regard to the budding global community. For World War II showed the world the immense destruction that modern warfare causes and provided a dramatic example in which the nations of the world would want to avoid at all costs in the future. The entire Cold War, following World War II, was in a sense a war that exemplified how to do everything possible to be in conflict without actually getting into *physical* conflict. The adjective "Cold" indicates that it was a war that was not fought in the ordinary sense of the word. The two nations at war never actually fought one another directly, except in a few minor and only recently discovered instances *(ex. Russian fighter pilots flew fighter jets during the Korean War against the UN & US forces)*.

Nuclear weapons also arose because of the incentive that the Second World War created to develop them. Now they exist as the most destructive force the world has known in many millions of years, since the last asteroid hit Earth. Hitler, by employing scientists to develop these weapons, provided the incentive for other nations to create them for defense, with little thought as to their long-term consequences.

It is arguably in large part because of the devastating capabilities of nuclear weapons that almost all of the most destructive and devastating wars occurred before World War II. America's involvement in today's conflicts in Iraq and Afghanistan where well over 1,000,000 troops have served and under 10,000 soldiers have died so far is dwarfed by that of World War II where 16,000,000 served and over 400,000 died. In the past and still today, war has served as a country's means of acquiring greater power and wealth; but today a war between two nuclear powers holds the potential of completely destroying both countries and their peoples. The conflict between India and Pakistan, whose conflicts have been going on since both were granted their independence from British rule in 1947, underwent a significant change in 1998 where both countries became nuclear powers. Since then only relatively minor and indirect fighting has occurred though tensions remain very high. It is believed by many that a balance has occurred where both nations are now too afraid to take any offensive measures.

Nuclear weapons are the ultimate instrument of war, for they are capable of delivering complete destruction. But the world, as seen partly from the India-Pakistan example, has in large part been forced into a peace because of nuclear weapons. The last sixty years, adjusting for population size, have been some of the most peaceful years the world has ever known, at least among most of the industrialized nations who have the nuclear weapons. Because of the fear induced by nuclear weapons, it seems unlikely, though not impossible, that a third world war will occur, unless started by accident. Although the possibility of nuclear war seems slim, an individual nuclear weapon detonating, due to terrorists, in a major city is higher than ever with nuclear weapon proliferation extending to smaller less stable countries.

The international organizations that exist today developed their foundations in the aftermath of World War II. The United

Nations was created as a means to ensure universal rights and peace for the world's nations—though, as with any human-created entity, it is far from perfect. Likewise, after World War I, it was thought that large-scale war was no longer a possibility because the war in Europe was so destructive. The League of Nations, like the UN, was supposed to maintain peace. With World War II these hopes were shattered by an even larger and more destructive war. However, such hopes have yet to be shattered since World War II.

Jesus, in direct contrast to Hitler, urged others to love and respect other people as in the Golden Rule: "Treat others as you would want to be treated yourself." Yet, regardless of how good an individual Jesus was, his influence upon the world might lead us to regard him as the individual responsible, however indirectly, for a larger number of killings than any other being ever to have walked the planet. But how?

To put Jesus' influence into perspective, the Bible has been the book with the greatest circulation ever since the invention of the printing press. In fact, it was the first book printed on the printing press! The Bible has influenced people both consciously and unconsciously to persecute and war against others all over the world in the name of the divisive ideology of the Bible. Human beings misconstrue the Bible because of their own emotions and ignorance. It is because of peoples' weaknesses that people have failed to faithfully follow Jesus' teachings which in themselves are good.

Divisions and conflict still abound because of contemporary Jesus followers, who are themselves, part of one of over 20,000 Christian sects in the world. It is the exclusiveness that Jesus' followers assign to their understanding of God that has caused so many divisions to occur among people across the globe. Such divisions are almost always the cause of conflict.

Jesus, regarded by many as the world's Savior and a messenger of love, can be considered, owing to his extreme influence over the ignorant masses, to be the most "evil" individual ever to have existed, because his life was and is the driving motivation behind more hate, conflict, and death than that

110

of any other individual throughout history. In the end, it is because of peoples' weaknesses that both Jesus and Hitler had so much power, and it is the extremity of their positions that, from a certain perspective, caused their life's deeds to be reversed after their deaths as in Newton's third law.

To take less extreme examples, many charitable foundations have been established after tragedies and disasters. After the Columbine tragedy, parents of one of the children created a scholarship program in one of the murdered student's name. Love, in the form of donations, poured into devastated areas after recent disasters such as the Southeast Asia tsunami, hurricane Katrina, and the terrorist attacks of 9/11. Compassion, love, heroism, and the desire for good are all spawned during and after tragedies.

Psychologically, human beings have many cycles, with some individuals having more pronounced or frequently occurring cycles than others. A person with a temperate personality has extremely mild cycles compared with a person with an intense personality.

One study showing the psychological tendency to alternate between extremes was conducted by two twentieth century psychologists, Schachter & Singer. In the study, they showed demonstrated that emotion needs two things present in order to exist: a physiologically aroused state and a cognitive label based upon the current environment which the individual is in. They conducted a study where subjects were injected with epinephrine inducing a physiologically aroused state. They then placed the subjects in a waiting room with either an angry or happy confederate, or person who was part of the experiment. The subjects' moods then became either positive or negative depending upon their environment. So, if one experiences a certain physiological state with no cognitive awareness of why it is occurring, the mind will try to find a reason enabling one to experience an emotion based upon that reason. Before a cognitive label can be placed upon the physiological state, the state itself is one of uneasiness, for it has no classification, and could be a result of one of two very different emotions.

111

Have you ever noticed how an angry or sad individual can suddenly swing to the other extreme? Anger and sadness both essentially result from a certain dissatisfaction, though anger is often associated with someone more aggressive and sadness with someone more passive. Have you also noticed how someone who is extremely happy can have their mood shattered in a moment when bad news arrives in whatever form, or vice versa? This is because the person, not maintaining a temperate frame of mind, allows their emotions to control their mind. This is not to say that there is not a time and a place, a "season," for each of these emotions, but it is why so many great people in history have considered temperance one of the most important virtues. Marcus Aurelius, a philosopher and Roman emperor, identified temperance as one of his four chief virtues, along with wisdom, fortitude, and justice.

One environment that lends itself quite well to the study of fluctuations of emotion is one in which a group of people get together and consume large amounts of alcohol. For alcohol upsets individuals' balanced systems and makes them more erratic and extreme. A person becomes either extremely loud or extremely quiet when drinking. He or she becomes either overly happy or overly angry and depressed.

For these reasons, let us consider an example associated with the system existing as nightclubs and bars. On one occasion, as I was taking the bus back home late at night, I overheard a female, who obviously had been drinking, crying to a friend because some guy had left her. Now the girl really was not crying because of the guy, but rather because of the void *left* by the guy. If she had never met the guy, she would never have experienced a void, where the guy used to reside, to cry over. This void leaves something to be filled within the emotional state of this individual, who like all of us seeks self-validation.

Suddenly a guy around the same age appears and, noticing the girl crying, approaches her. Both individuals within this system have desired ends: The girl wants to fill the void within her, and the guy wants to fill his own voids. After a few minutes of "consoling" the girl, astonishingly, her tears suddenly turn to laughter, because the void within her extremely emotional state had been filled at least temporarily in this state of mind, causing her to be "validated" once again, with little prompting from the guy. Likewise, the infamous "on the rebound" state in people who have just recently broken up with a significant other causes a strong vacuum within the person due to extreme emotions that occur during this time period. The person seeks validation even with people they ordinarily would not have been attracted to.

Another somewhat famous example of extremes going to the other extreme is what we might call the yo-yo diet, which involves an all-or-nothing approach to eating properly. In this diet, the individual is motivated for whatever reason to begin a strict diet starting from a planned day—sometimes the same day the decision is made to go on a diet. At this point, he or she will completely alter their diet, allowing no junk food at all. In essence, they build a dam holding back their craving for food but make no allowance for the cravings they will undoubtedly feel—no outlet enabling the cravings to be released. In the all-or-nothing diet there is no controlled flooding of the dam, which would allow for some of these cravings to be alleviated, easing the process.

So now the person who has been accustomed to eating whatever they want, whenever they want, will experience what seem to be uncontrollable urges to eat food that they do not allow in their diet. This diet, then, constitutes an extremely trying test of their will power. The craving for their old junk food will arise again once the initial novelty of the diet has worn off, causing the dam to spring a leak.

This first leak may be prompted by a person offering them some food, or a late-night interlude wherein the refrigerator is "calling" the person to give in to temptation, or the arrival of bad news. At first this leak may be small and repairable, as is the case if the person decides to have just one piece of chocolate. One piece of chocolate is hardly a bad thing in itself for a person who has been eating well for the past several days; but this piece of chocolate, if not allowed for—as in the controlled flooding of a dam represents a leak in will power. Any leak will naturally tend to become a larger leak—often very fast, as chaos attempts to destroy order. This larger leak will be much more difficult to repair and at one point will become irreparable, as is the case with the individual who, after eating that one piece of chocolate, finds himself sick to his stomach after eating the whole box.

Like people, the atmosphere also has cycles as different regions at different times become more or less pressurized. When there is a pocket of low pressure, that region does not have as many air molecules. Therefore, when a high-pressure pocket with a higher concentration of molecules passes next to a low-pressure region it will tend to flood into the low-pressure region, causing wind. In general, the greater the contrast between the two regions' pressures, the greater the winds will be, for polar extremes when they meet tend to provoke extreme reactions. The common expression, "The calm before the storm," represents this contrast.

The same holds true with respect to temperature. An area of heated water will tend to disperse into colder water, and vice versa. The heated area's excited molecules will lose energy to the colder area's molecules, with the overall system attempting to reach equilibrium.

The stock market, real estate, and other investments are well plotted systems of cycles. Obviously, the reason why these systems are well charted is because they were created by human beings and individual stocks for example have finite amounts of shares and prices. The stock market has been charted since its conception and has been a relatively good gauge as to how a particular nation is doing.

Despite the fact that the stock market is well charted, it is obviously difficult to predict due to the many variables influencing it, especially since people, who are the reason for its advances and declines, are extrinsically motivated to know the cycles existing within it. A system aware of itself as being a system no longer knows the way, or patterns, of that system. Jean-Paul Sartre puts it this way:

114

As soon as we posit ourselves as a certain being, by a legitimate judgment, based on inner experience or correctly deduced from a priori or empirical premises, then by that very positing we surpass this being. . . .

So in large part, the vast amount of uncertainty in all social science realms, including such disciplines as psychology, sociology, political science, and economics, is due to the fact that human beings have a self-reflective consciousness. Thus the stock market has patterns, but these patterns are often not as well pronounced as other cycles, because the controlling elements of the system and its patterns are aware of them. Because of this awareness, the moment a pattern arises and is discovered by the elements within the system it becomes altered on account of that recognition, and because of the subsequent adaptation that the individuals aware of the pattern make in order to capitalize on it. The Tao Te Ching says, "What everyone knows is not knowledge, what no one knows is."

Looking at the stock market after the September 11, 2001, World Trade Center attack, it is very easy to understand the significant drop in stock prices across almost all industries, except for the security industry, which skyrocketed. The otherwise relatively stable, inert system experienced a very large disturbance to its usual relative balance. It was acted upon by a very large outside force, including peoples' fears, and therefore was pushed into motion, changing it. September 11 spurred a cycle that resembles many others throughout the history of the stock market. Any time a disaster of one sort or another occurs, the people and the world react. This reaction follows a pattern that can be known and utilized.

Another, though different, example are the "peaks and valleys" within one's mind that are caused by drugs. The immediate effect of the most commonly taken illicit, and some prescription, drugs is a sensation of overall euphoria due to the internal mechanisms of the brain being artificially stimulated. Once the initial "high" dissipates, however, the system, trying to reach stasis or equilibrium, responds by going to the opposite extreme. The brain seeks to stabilize itself, which involves the user going from a "high" to a point much lower than the "high," causing the user's mood to drop. This "low" hooks many people into taking the drug again, in search of a new "high" and because they are trying to maintain a non-depressed state. With repeated use of the drug, however, the user's equilibrium, which their mood usually fluctuates around, drops to lower than normal levels, depressing the entire system. Each subsequent use therefore makes the "high" less high and the "low" more low, causing a spiraling downward cycle.

The excitation levels of the neurons involved can not constantly be firing, and must rest at some point. In general, high activity leads to low activity and low activity leads to high activity. But as with everything, high and low activity levels are relative. For a marathon runner, high activity may be running ten miles in the morning, whereas for a television-watching couch potato it may be doing a little cleaning around the house. For an iron (Fe) atom, high activity may be being heated to several hundred degrees Celsius, whereas for a hydrogen (H) atom it may be attained around zero degrees Celsius; at both temperatures the respective element turns into a gas.

High activity levels cannot be sustained in and of themselves; some external force has to sustain the activity. In humans, it is the calories and various ingredients within the food we eat, while in atoms it may be the sun exciting their electrons.

Likewise, there must be rest for there to be motion in the vast majority of entities on Earth. A person who walks while eating non-stop along the way will eventually be unable to continue because even though the person has available energy due to the food, the muscle tissue will accumulate tears to the point where the tissue is no longer usable.

The molecule at rest with low activity levels will tend to stay at rest, but at the same time it lends itself as an outlet for the energy that other, high-energy molecules have built up. The cold item will tend to become hot; the hot item will tend to become cold.

When a molecule of sodium chloride (NaCl) is formed, the relationship between Na and Cl will be balanced, with both elements' properties being moderated but still expressed, since both elements are of near-equal size and possess compatible qualities. But when two elements bind and one has much stronger properties than the other, the weaker one's properties may be dominated by the stronger one such as in Uranium Trioxide (UO_3) where the heavy Uranium atom dominates much of the molecules' properties.

Finally, as human beings and as animals in general, we are usually somewhat shortsighted in our perspectives. How could we *not* be, when our lives are so short and when our bodies demand constant attention to remain in working order? This shortsightedness poses an interesting dilemma for human beings. For inasmuch as there are cycles existing over long periods of time, such as Earth's periodic ice ages, are human beings living unawares in our own vast cycle? Starting with the first human beings around a million years ago, fighting to survive, avoiding predation, and then gradually progressing through the initial stages of technology, politics, social organization, and the like, are we, through technology, destined to overcome the "evils" of the world, balancing out the sheer struggle to survive with a life in the future that today exists only in our dreams as an ideal—as utopia? Or are we destined to disappear from the planet as we once appeared on it?

Putting It All Together . . . Seeing Patterns through Cycles

Patterns in the System that arise as fluctuations between dualities exist as cycles. The unseen cycles are often expressed visually as patterns, such as the branching of tree branches, blood vessels, and rivers or the swirls of milk in coffee and distant galaxies.

Cycles are responsible for the shaping of everything within the constantly fluctuating System. You were created within a reproductive cycle, which was and in many cases still is influenced by the seasons, which were influenced by the Earth's

117

cycle around the Sun and its own rotation cycle.

Cycles exist only because of dualities. Without duality, cycles would not be able to exist for cycling around one pole is impossible and becomes a static system. Sorrow without happiness knows no mode of being other than sorrow and would cease to *be* sorrow, for what is sorrow but the opposite of happiness? Sorrow existing by itself would simply be the way things are. Jean-Paul Sartre says, "Being can not exist without nothingness, for without nothingness the very idea of being is impossible."

Knowing about cycles allows one to put things into context. Life and the world always encounter ups and downs. Knowledge of cycles is vital to understanding yourself. Everyone is composed of an infinite number of internal cycles, from neurotransmitter/hormonal fluctuations and the beating of your heart to the replicating of your DNA within individual cells and the firing of one particular neuron within your brain due to swings in your mood.

Perhaps the most poignant cycles to us as human beings are those we can't escape from even though we are aware of their patterns. We have one continuous cycle of life, in which conception begins our existence and death ends it. In between, we undergo so many major cycles and stages. After we are birthed we are babies who strive to reach childhood. After childhood we strive to reach adolescence and young adulthood. As adults we have reached the pinnacle of our development as we either fight against or accept growing older. We watch the next generations of humans who are at stages that we once were at, as they progress into adults: our children and grandchildren, giving us new life by giving us hope in them. Those who fear death also fear life. For life has been paid for in full through our inevitable death.

VI.

Who, What, Why, Where, & How...
Words of investigation

"As Cuvier could correctly describe a whole animal by the contemplation of a single bone, so the observer who has thoroughly understood one link in a series of incidents, should be able accurately to state all of the other ones, both before and after."

- Sherlock Holmes

Who, What, Why, Where, & How are necessary words through which to learn. For although all of the basic principles to understand everything were discussed in the preceding chapters, in order to actually utilize them one must ask questions about them as well as about the world around them. After all, cliché as it may sound, a question unasked is a question unanswered. The seed unplanted is the seed that remains a seed.

One may know many things but will never be able to progress in their knowledge if it just sits unexplored. Like the ancient Chinese proverb says, "That which stops growing is that which starts dying," which is also expressed in Bob Dylan's song "It's Alright, Ma (I'm Only Bleeding)." Jump-started by curiosity, a person's knowledge may interact with itself to yield more knowledge—and such knowledge is more powerful and more memorable than that taught by another. For it is your own knowledge; self-created, grounded in many connections within the mind instead of a few outside it. Descartes said:

119

If I feel that I can learn something through my own
faculties, I will avoid learning it through other means, so
that I may have the simple pleasure of reveling
in this capability that I possess.

And anything that yields beneficial results—whether it be a well-performing car, a good pen, a successful crop, or a special skill—is something that will be returned to time and time again.

The love of ideas and learning needs to be stoked and rekindled. Anything that is loved is desired. Anything that is loved is returned to with an open heart. And as John Wooden said, "Perfect practice makes perfect." Questioning the world is good, but it must be done with an open, unclouded mind if it is to yield the closest thing we can get to the truth, and subsequently to understanding everything. Everything has a reason for being within the System; everything has its beginning and end. The height of questioning is when you question the world while questioning yourself. The two have become one.

Skepticism: The Art of Questioning Humanity

The need for artful questioning is especially pronounced when it comes to interacting with other human beings in a society where everyone is trying to survive. Advertisements, which are the essence of deception and manipulation, abound in this capitalistic world. People call on the phone asking you to spare just a couple of minutes in order that they may persuade you to buy some product or service. Today's human being has perfected the art of deception: playing upon peoples' desire to fulfill their particular goals. No matter how morally upstanding an individual is, no one is beyond the use of this craft. It is both our strength and our weakness.

In our dichotomous system, we as living beings exist between two polarities. The idea of pure good or evil is much like the idealistic geometrical shapes that the ancient Greeks created. Neither exists in the natural world. They are ideals.

One should therefore realize that everything is not always as it appears. Even as one seeks the truth, one must understand that the truth lies within deceptions, both within the mind and outside it.

So let us return to the example used in the Dualities discussion in Chapter 4, dealing with the advertisement on the platform of an underground (subway) station. A gigantic ad, you will remember, consisting of a photograph of the bluest of blue oceans and skies, with a little sliver of white beach and a palm tree. Imposed on this background was a girl splashing water toward the viewer, who takes up one-third of the ad and who is tan, gorgeous, and wearing only a skimpy bikini. The words "Experience the warmth of this sun-baked land" appear at the top. Yet the advertisement, advertising the beauty of Turkey to the commuter traffic of London, showed curiously little of Turkey itself. Why?

To understand the ad, one must first understand the audience for the ad. The individual living in the system existing as London lives in an environment that is cold, foggy, and damp, especially during the winter months. So what do the people of this area want? The opposite.

The sun and the blue skies on the ad are two things heavily associated with life, since it is the sun that provides the energy for nearly every living entity on Earth. However, in a London winter the number of days with sun and blue skies is so few that one may find oneself taking a picture of a landscape (as I have done) just because a rare piece of blue sky has become visible.

So why would the ad show a fuller representation of Turkey when the audience it is advertising to, and trying to lure *to* Turkey, is starved for sun and warmth? Seeing the bluest of blue skies, white sandy beaches, and scantily clad bronzed women is vastly more attractive to a Londoner than seeing some distinctive building in Turkey—London already *has* many buildings—and the words chosen for the ad (warmth, sun, baked) reinforce these images.

Why does a gorgeous girl take up one-third of an

advertisement promoting Turkey? Does the girl represent Turkey that well? Probably less than one-half of one percent of the women in Turkey look like this girl. So, in the end, the advertisers are playing upon the weary businessman's psyche, enticing him away from the long day's work ahead into a fantasy world in his mind that is not truth. The women, too, are enticed by the ad which promises them an exotic, attractive looking sun tan from relaxing on an exotic beach. London commuters are offered a representation of the opposite of everything they are weary of in London. The marketers who made this ad knew their audience. They knew how to manipulate the strings of their Underground traveler marionettes so that, first and foremost, they would profit. They laid a trap to catch their food.

One of the most important things to understand is what the real advertiser or communicator, in this case the Turkish tourism council wants from their communications: money. In order to *get* money, they need to lure people to Turkey. All advertisements aim to persuade through one means or another, without regard for the truth. They are selling something—an image, an illusion—and they will use every possible tactic to get you to buy what it is they are selling. They know you in some ways better than you know yourself. They will show and tell you anything you want to see or hear, just so long as, in the end, they get their money.

But we *all* exist as advertisements. Human beings, like all animals, fall under the same principles that operate within the framework of evolution. We all need to survive and fulfill certain innate needs. We have evolved so that in many cases our primary concerns are not with the ends, such as food, shelter, or mating partners, but rather with the means, as in money and power, which allow us to fulfill all of our physical and a few of our psychological needs, in order to adapt and thrive.

Even morality is a form of deception. Morality is a construction of the human mind that for the past several millennia has provided society as a whole with a means to achieve its desired ends by increasing order and decreasing chaos. Morality benefits individuals in several ways, including building trust with others, enabling the creation of beneficial bonds that can be utilized for survival, and boosting people's mental health by improving their image of themselves. Morality is an abstract tool humanity has used to advance itself. It can be likened to the piece of grass that chimpanzees have learned to use to get termites from inside a deep hole, or the rocks that sea otters use to open abalone. It is a survival adaptation developed by the human species. Morality serves as constraint imposed by society in order to allow it to grow in a stable form, by imposing rules upon the humans within who are ultimately concerned with their own success.

There is not a single person who is not, whether consciously or unconsciously, like the ad in the underground station. People are always trying to sell themselves. Whether it is to acquire money or friends, happiness or self-validation or sex, people are always selling themselves to others. There are no exceptions.

Buddhism, along with some other religions, holds that desire is one of the ultimate evils. The reason Buddhists try to eliminate desire is that desire creates a void within the individual that eventually leads to unhappiness because of the perceived lack of fulfillment. Now, when people are in a state of unhappiness, they exist in a state that is highly susceptible to manipulation, for they want their unhappiness to be relieved. This is where advertisers flourish.

Imagine having no place to live in a foreign country and looking for an apartment. There is a void within, looking to be filled. The landlord of one of the places you view hears your accent and immediately knows that you are from America. This deeply in-debt individual then goes on a long monologue about how much he loves America. Now, in all likelihood, this person does not walk around London talking about his "love of America," especially during a time period when America is unpopular. But you were looking for a place to stay, and the landlord was looking for someone to rent his empty apartment and provide him with sustenance to live. Therefore, he plays with your emotions by evoking the good feelings that you have, and almost anyone has, for their country of origin, especially when traveling in a foreign land.

Just like the landlord, many people who want something will try to relate to their "prey" as if (s)he were one of their own. The veritable wolf covered in sheep's wool. They initiate conversations by asking your name, where you are from, and what your interests are. They then subtly, and deceptively depict an external reality that the individual most certainly will desire.

Robert Cialdini, the social psychologist and father of persuasion, identifies six such influence tactics that can hypnotize the most aware of individuals in the right circumstances: reciprocation, commitment and consistency, social proof, liking, authority, and scarcity. All of these tactics help to obscure the truth, and are therefore important to understand in order to undermine their manipulative power over oneself.

Let's briefly review these influence tactics now. Reciprocation's power is the result of the feeling of indebtedness that we get when we are given something. We feel that we must reciprocate to the person who gave us something by giving them something in return. This has been a standard social practice for thousands of years that has built relations between different groups of people such as two different tribes or countries.

Commitment and consistency's power arise as a natural result of the human mind's need for a consistent image of itself. Commitment engages this need of the mind by making the person choose a path while consistency induces a need for the person to stay on that path. The integrity gained through consistent behavior allows us to develop the best possible relations with others.

Social proof's power arises from the benefits that fitting into the group gives the individual. Social acceptance has many survival benefits in not only our species but others. Social behavior provides protection, acquisition of resources, mating partners, and companions. We learn how to be human by watching others, and all one needs to see this instinct is by observing how a child will imitate those around them. If others are doing it, that behavior must be correct.

Liking almost needs no explanation. We are influenced by those individuals and things that we like. Physical attractiveness, similarities, and cooperation are just a few of the things that influence something's likeability.

The very essence of authority is that it has the power to control and influence. It is built into our understanding of the world that we listen to those with authority-the authority of our parents, teachers, police, and others. We are told who is in charge of everything, and most often we choose to follow.

Lastly, scarcity influences since that which is scarce usually is valuable. Part of the very essence of economics is based upon this principle. The smaller the supply of a resource, the higher the demand and therefore the higher the price will be.

Why do people wear their best clothes when they go out or attend special events? Why does it matter if one wears a thousand-dollar Armani jacket as opposed to an old twenty-dollar Kmart special? The two jackets may and undoubtedly do feel different, but in general they both accomplish the same end of keeping the wearer warm. What pleasure or satisfaction does one derive, therefore, from wearing the Armani? Part of the answer lies within the wearer—but the other part lies within those who *view* the wearer.

The Armani-wearing individual wants to look good so as to feel better about himself when meeting with other people. In this case, he derives benefit from wearing the jacket through the knowledge that he looks good while in the presence of others. Thus his sense of self is reinforced, assuaging his insecurities through the knowledge that the jacket he wears holds some sort of power over others. But the Armani-wearing individual is marketing himself to himself as well, the jacket acting as a drug. The moment he puts on the Armani he internalizes its qualities, as if it was food for his ego. The jacket nourishes his self-confidence and makes him look better.

With regard to others, the individual is, again, marketing himself. The Armani wearer will be looked upon much more favorably than the Kmart-special wearer. It is the image that the jacket portrays that attracts others, because people enjoy being around those whom they perceive as having positive qualities which they too would like to have, or to have reinforced. Just as an animal that has just made a large kill attracts others, a person with money attracts people. After all, you are whom you are friends with.

An Armani jacket is much like the plumage of a peacock. Peacocks are able or unable to attract females in large part on account of how beautiful their feathers are. If a peacock has beautiful feathers it will display them proudly to any passing peacocks, trying to attract potential mates and repel possible competitors. The male wants to do everything possible to make his potential mates feel good about their decision to bear his children by submitting to him.

Peoples' clothes, like the peacock's plumage, act as an advertisement, giving others a quick, instant impression of who the person is. Ever notice the way a person walking in a business suit walks a little bit taller than everyone else? Their egos have been artificially inflated.

Now imagine the same individual stranded on a deserted island. What benefit could be derived from a jacket now, except as a means to keep warm? The social element—the marketing element—has been eliminated, as there no longer is an audience. In such a situation, the effect of the Armani jacket would undoubtedly be greatly reduced since the social element has been removed.

The heavy-set Gaboon viper lies in wait for its prey as it blends ever so delicately into the leafy forest floor. The Angler fish lures its prey in the dark depths of the ocean by turning on a built-in light, which it flashes so as to mesmerize its potential prey amid the darkness. Some ground-nesting mother birds, such as the killdeer, engage in a broken-wing display where they will act as if injured, leaving the nest making themselves as conspicuous as possible to predators presenting them with a pseudo-opportunity—and drawing them away from the camouflaged chicks, which are their true opportunity.

People possess minds of considerably more depth than

any other animal. Our deceptions are so deceptive and subtle as to be in many cases unknown even to ourselves. Why is it that teenagers go through fads so rapidly, changing what they like every month or so? Marketers know the susceptibility of this unstable age. Why is it that in general peoples' living spaces are so full of useless junk that merely collects dust? Marketing creates needs or voids that otherwise are not present.

Deception is all around us and takes on many forms. The girl wearing an extra-heavy coat of makeup deceives her unobservant audience into believing that she has perfect skin. The very clothes we wear enable us, like the octopus, the chameleon, and the moth, to change colors and even form. The cars we drive, the music we listen to, portray to the external world, and therefore to ourselves, an image of who we are, whether we really *are* that image or not. The overweight guy walking his pit bull down the street, arms outstretched not because of his muscles but because of his immense amount of fat seems to walk as if he is the toughest individual on the planet. He undoubtedly internalizes the breed's qualities into his image of himself and hopes they will adhere to him in everyone else's minds as well. The girl wearing the trendy hat that she just saw in the latest hip-hop video is trying to quiet her immense insecurities by internalizing the qualities of the gorgeous girls in the videos. She too hopes that everyone else will think about her the way she does when wearing that hat. But in both of these instances, these people in essence are still the same person, with or without the pit bull or the trendy hat. As Henry David Thoreau put it:

A goose is still a goose,
whether wearing swan feathers or not.

Life is too finite to not actually live it in truth. The worst deceptions are those that are self-created and imposed upon ourselves, creating delusions that could fall apart at any moment. Don't become the unsuspecting fish that gets gobbled up by the angler fish. The fish that is aware of the deception is the fish that is aware of itself.

Questioning the Natural World

Everything in the world has a reason. It is only our ignorance that blinds us from the truth.

Let's look at an example of how to question an unknown entity. Walking along a trail in certain parts of the United States, one may come across clusters of little bubbles attached to the stalks of wild grasses. What are these? Who made them? Why were they made? When were they made? The answer to just one of these questions can lead to the answers for all of them.

Upon closer examination, several small green insects are resting on the stalks next to these bubble structures. It may then be concluded with some level of certainty that these creatures are somehow associated to these structures. But how?

Observation reveals that the green insects have released this bubbly material as one does so right before my eyes. But to what end is it doing this? Consider the basic life cycle of any organism: life and, eventually, death, with the imperatives of fulfilling needs for food, shelter, and reproduction in between. The bubble structures could then be some sort of trap to obtain food. But the bubbles are not that sticky, and the insect itself looks far from formidable in terms of being any sort of predator that would feed upon others. So in all likelihood, the structures do not exist to capture food.

They could be shelters, for many animals have unique structures that one may not immediately think of as such (One such example is the bubble nest shelter created by one-type of water spider, which creates an air pocket under ponds and other bodies of water). But this structure seems too inaccessible to be a shelter, for the insect would have to wade through this bubbly muck in order to get in and out.

So out of the basic needs of life, we are left with the possibility that they might have to do with reproduction. But how? There is no visible mating occurring. Yet all other reasonable options seem to be ruled out.

It seems, therefore, that these numerous sessile and

128

unguarded structures are some sort of nest. Closer examination reveals, after picking apart one of the structures, there is a small developing green insect that looks much like the ones surrounding the structures, except in an immature form. These must then be egg structures of these green insects.

Field guides later verified our answer. Answering our question regarding what the bubble sacs were was simply a matter of methodical questioning in conjunction with application of the basic principles of the natural world.

Another question we might ask is what is the range of these insects? One could always infer the range by assuming that this insect and other similar insects probably also live in locations where the habitats are similar. But if one were to apply this reasoning, for example, to rats, which live virtually everywhere, one might be misled. The art of inference is one of reasoned generalization.

Now there are some aspects of these insects that cannot be discovered by investigation in the absence of outside information. Their name for example, the North American Treehopper, would have been extremely difficult to arrive at only by observation even though it is somewhat of a transparent name. For even though it is true that they do noticeably hop, and that they live in North America and may even be seen in trees, they could just as easily have been named after the species discoverer.

As another example, imagine if one were to see a polar bear for the first time in a zoo. Upon visual inspection of the animal, it could be inferred that it must live in cold climates on account of its heavy, white (which is actually clear) coat of fur, which would blend into such an environment, where it needs to sneak up on unsuspecting prey. A factor that would be difficult to surmise with such a superficial inspection is the fact that the fur is actually clear allowing light to shine through, hitting its black skin which absorbs the light's heat.

Looking at a map of the British Isles, located halfway up the Northern hemisphere, much can be inferred about the particular environments existing upon these islands as well as the ocean's circulatory systems of the North Atlantic that affect them. Looking at the coasts on these islands, one can see a pattern of erosion. How did this pattern come to be, and what does it mean for the islands themselves?

First, the Earth revolves in an eastwardly direction, which could be inferred, if it was not known already, by observing on which side the sun rises and sets. This eastwardly rotation causes the general flow of water and air currents, which are intricately related, to flow in the same direction. Knowing that, in general, the Earth's currents flow west to east, it can be inferred that the significant erosion resulting in the numerous inlets on the west coasts of Ireland and the United Kingdom are due to these eastwardly currents. However, consider the intricacies of the land as the currents are channeled into the Irish Sea between the islands of Ireland and Britain. Notice how the middle portion of Britain is carved out. Now notice the swirling motion that occurs when one pours milk into coffee, the motion of hurricanes, or galaxies. The land in this region is carved out largely because of such swirling of water currents, which had become trapped in between the two land masses.

Based on its northerly longitude, one can guess what the vegetation on the land here would be, particularly if one knows the vegetation in regions of similar longitude. For example, no cactuses or palm trees would exist, for these plants' structures, characterized by a small surface area-to-mass ratio, are conducive to water conservation—which is not an advantage in areas of this longitude. Areas this far north are almost always moist. Also, since it is the west coast of both islands that is exposed to heavy water and air currents, inducing heavy erosion, it can be assumed that these coasts would have a greater tendency to have cliffs.

Upon further investigation this does indeed prove to be the case, with the renowned Cliffs of Moher existing on the west coast of Ireland as well as the mountainous nation of Wales, part of the United Kingdom. So since the west coasts are cliffs, the east coasts, in general, could be expected to have more level shores because they are secluded from currents as well as to the natural tendency for opposites to exist within systems. This is also the case in the United States, where the West Coast has a deep drop-off into the Pacific Ocean whereas the East has beaches with much gentler gradations.

Additionally, given the flow of currents, our knowledge of the Earth's rotation, and the existence of various land masses in the North Atlantic, one could predict which route a plane or boat will take when traveling to these islands from North America. Even today, with advanced technology and jet engines, traveling these age-old routes produced by water and air currents, airlines and boating companies reduce both traveling time and fuel usage, thereby fulfilling both the travelers' needs and their own needs. A desirable route can be identified before traveling by observing the patterns that the Earth presents to its inhabitants, for the Earth presents a way of being, grounded in the overall System, which remains intact regardless of human inventions. It is always easier to follow the flow of things presented by the System.

Imagine an investigator who is tracking an individual. By using techniques similar to those described above, if the investigator knows where the individual lives and works, (s)he can predict with a high degree of accuracy what route the individual will take everyday to work, in accordance with several other factors such as roads, traffic, and the person's personality. Each piece of information adds to the investigator's likelihood of discovering the truth.

Now, look at a car and its many parts. Why does it need so many elements to run? This question may be easiest to answer by asking, "Why does the human body have so many parts?" For the basic principles underlying a car and the human body are essentially the same. If one knows the structure of the human body, one then knows to a large extent the structure of the automobile. Both need fuel, existing as gasoline and food, respectively; both need oxygen to combust or metabolize this fuel, and both need cooling systems to vent excess heat to prevent damage to each ones internals.

With respect to acquiring clean air, the car has an air filter which circles the air intake valve, keeping the engine clean of contaminants that could damage it. The nose (that is, the air intake valve of a human being) has an intricate structure built to take air into one's lungs while filtering out contaminants by means of nose hairs, a mucous lining just inside the nasal cavity, and the like. The nose unlike the car's air intake valve which acquires air through the motion of the car, needs the lungs to pump air into the body. By knowing one thing, one need only ask questions and use reason to know many things.

Putting It All Together: Question Everything

Sherlock Holmes, the world's most famous and successful detective, is excellent at deducing facts by asking the right questions about the situations he encounters that he is able to solve almost every case. Of course, part of his success arises from the fact that he is fictional, and that his creator, Arthur Conan Doyle, plans his victories for him in advance. From a more analytical standpoint, however, it is his constant questioning, his vast foundation of knowledge, and his awareness that everything in the world has a reason for being the way it is at any given moment that allows him to see what others do not. As Holmes points out to Watson:

You see, but you do not observe.

A book resting on top of a nightstand with a certain amount of dust on top of it can be inferred to have been there for a particular period of time corresponding to the room's overall dustiness. The leaves from a particular type of tree, strewn across the rooftop and blown there by currents originating miles away; the worn-down carpet right by the doorway—these, too, are clues that can yield more information about their respective systems.

By asking questions one may not always receive specifics back, but generalizations lead to specifics when the right questions are asked. As we have stated many times before, knowledge processed through thought begets more knowledge.

132

Questions also act as a survival tool to make one aware of danger, whether the danger of being killed or just of being deceived. For as the clichéd saying goes, "The only stupid question is the question unasked." A question's purpose is to eliminate the question, just as the purpose of hunger is to impel the organism to eat food so that hunger will be eliminated. A question's purpose is to metamorphose into an answer. The moment an answer is found, it springs forth with all of the beauty that only the truth can hold. Truth allows one to transcend their current condition. Sartre says,

The consciousness is ever trying to transcend itself, pushing away from what it is not but is, in the form of being attached to a body.

Questions are consciousness' means to transcendence.

VII.

The Parts become the Whole...
principles of the whole.

*"In the unitive state one sees without seeing,
for there is nothing separate from him;
smells without smelling; hears without
hearing; feels without feeling; & tastes without tasting."*

- The Upanishads

THE PARTS BECOME THE WHOLE as one
acquires an understanding of everything. The whole is nothing
more than a composition of its parts, and the parts are nothing
more than elements of the whole. Without a beginning there
could be no end; without an end is there a beginning?

So it is, as with all things, that this book now must enter
its winter. And as in winter, this book will reflect upon that
which has already been said. Now that all of the essential
components for understanding the world in its entirety at a
general level have been introduced, this chapter will try to unite
them, and to explore several principles concerning these elements
that will help maximize one's understanding of them—and,
subsequently, of everything.

In learning or perfecting anything, it is the fundamentals

that teachers and coaches always return to in teaching their students. It is the ground floor from which one exits a skyscraper. It is addition and subtraction that are returned to in mathematics when one is doing differential equations. The fundamentals make up the complex. The complex, therefore, follows the way of the fundamentals.

In congruence with the point of the last chapter, everything should be looked upon skeptically, for many contradictions exist within generalities. But for entities of our infinitely minute size, the world exists as one large, inconceivable generality and contradiction, for every point has its counterpoint. As Walt Whitman said:

Do I contradict myself?
Very well then . . . I contradict myself;
I am large . . . I contain multitudes.

But generalities or fundamentals are valuable in the sense that they are similar across disciplines, whereas the specifics are often very different. Specifics are so complex as to be unknowable with our current brains.

Awareness of one's mind is foundational. The mind is a filter through which everything is perceived, interpreted, and known; a clouded, undisciplined mind filled with biases distorts the truth. For this reason, knowledge of one's mind is essential. Some build their castles on stilts, only to discover that their castles never really existed, as they watch their worlds come crashing down upon themselves.

Awareness of divisions and classifications allows one to appreciate the human conventions that shape and control one's perceptions and one's thoughts about things. A scent trail that ants follow is no different than a sidewalk that people follow, a highway full of cars, or blood cells in a vein. They are all paths of transportation for different entities within the world following very similar patterns. Divisions and classifications allow for the organization of complex ideas and information into an easily understandable format for use by people and other animals. How do we know friend from foe, mate from rival, or food from poison?

Awareness of *systems* allows one to see the interactions between all things within the one overall, all-containing System. Everything exists in a unique relationship to everything else, each component affecting the other. This idea is similar to the famous "butterfly effect" of chaos theory, whereby the flap of a butterfly's wings in Thailand can result in a hurricane half a world away in Florida. Everything is connected to and dependent upon the other elements within its own particular systems.

Awareness of the dualities existing within the System allows one to know the spectrum of possibilities that lie between the two extremes that compose systems. Nothing exists within the System that is other than dualistic in essence.

Awareness of cycles caused by flux within dualistic systems is important in order to understand changes within a system. All systems undergo a cycle of some sort. People themselves undergo an infinite number of internal cycles, caused by physiological entities or by the mind's response to both internal and external stimuli. These cycles shape our perceptions of the world.

Awareness of the power of skepticism and questioning allows one to infer knowledge from previous knowledge by asking the right questions concerning one's own mind and regarding divisions and classifications, systems, dualities, and cycles. Everything has a reason for being as it currently is, was, and will be.

The ability to understand everything is not a computer-like ability; it is a free-flowing, organic ability. The narrative in Chapter 0 is a good example of the non-rigid structure that characterizes the mind that is able to understand everything. Such flexibility is necessary because of our ability to "see" only one item in our consciousness at any one time. Therefore understanding everything must be a gradual process of building, moment by moment and nugget of knowledge by nugget of knowledge, until many such have accumulated, accessible at a moment's notice within one's mind. When a sufficient level of knowledge has been reached, if one lets go of their normally attentive mind and just focuses on the void existing as everything, an overwhelming sense of knowing overtakes one's Self. At such a moment, an individual can feel like a deity, as all things become one . . . which they were all along.

All the Same; All Different

Everything in the world is the same; everything in the world is different. Profound, huh? It is. Many examples have been given throughout this book highlighting the similarities between different elements of the world. It is only in the specifics that things differ.

This concept has been stated for millennia, with each new generation rehashing it in a different form for that particular era. In *Leviathan*, Hobbes compares the political system to a giant monster whose body parts are compared to different elements of the government. In *Cybernetics*, Norbert Wiener compares animals and their internal functioning to that of computers and machines.

Human beings in general are all the same. We all exist in the same System, in which we are born and then die; we all have the same fundamental needs and desires, and have bodies that have roughly the same physiology. There are many superficial differences, however, in our appearances, body structures, blood types, DNA, and the like but fundamentally these are just nuances *(Albeit, nuances can sometimes be of utmost importance. In genetically passed on maladies or diseases, problems may be caused by only a few links in the DNA)*. Our brains, too, have different structures and contain different connections between neurons as a result of past experiences, chemical imbalances, genetics, and the information and knowledge we possess. At heart, though, we are all the same.

Newton's concept of inertia applies to all things, not just the physical interactions that he had in mind. Once seated on a couch, for example, an individual is unlikely to move, for an object at rest will stay at rest unless acted upon. Maybe someone calls you over, or you get a sensation of hunger and go to the refrigerator; or maybe after a period of time an internal motivation is built up to move again because you need to stretch and move your muscles. The idea is the same, however, whether the force that gets you to move is an earthquake, someone pushing you, an internal drive, or nothing more than words. You need to have some force acting upon you for you to move or for that matter, to do anything.

A relatively balanced ecological system will tend to remain in a somewhat balanced state of inertia unless acted upon by an outside force. Maybe an exotic species is introduced into the environment. Depending upon the strength of the species or its adaptability in this new environment, the new species could act as a gigantic force kicking the ecosystem out of its relatively balanced state, or its effect could be negligible, because it is unable to survive and dies out.

Take organisms' behavior in general. At the most basic level, human beings are no different than single-celled bacteria that reproduce sexually. Like them, we need a habitable environment, a source of energy, internal mechanisms enabling us to convert food into energy, a system that allows us to recognize danger, an outlet for waste products, and mates in order to reproduce so that we can pass on our genes.

Consider a flock of pigeons pecking around at the sidewalk. One of these pigeons is puffing up its dewlap under its neck, showing off its marbled purple coloration as it rhythmically bobs its head up and down, circling around a duller-colored pigeon. Now go to a dance club and notice the same behavior being enacted by human beings. Both are mating rituals, though they have their own respective, species-specific components. Human beings, having a more complex brain—thereby gifted or cursed, depending upon your perspective—elaborate this ritual to a more complex state, involving different types of dances and such. But the basics—the ends—are still the same, masked only by the means. The pigeon has his purple plumage; the human being has a collared shirt or miniskirt. The idea is the same.

If you read a book about training dogs, you

139

simultaneously learn how to train children or significant others. Obviously the specifics are different, but the basic principles are the same. Always be consistent in your training, otherwise the one being trained will become confused, and their behavior will be erratic. Small, unexpected treats provide considerable motivation and reinforcement, whether they are compliments or dog biscuits.

Politics exists within the animal kingdom, as is the case with gorillas. Termites and ants have a complex social system constructed around members engaged in division of labor.

Ants release scent trails leading to and from their homes as a means of a scout leading the colony to a source of food. Although people do not use scent trails like ants, because of differing sensory capabilities, we do, on account of our visually dominated perceptual system, build roads with lines painted on them to direct us. People rarely wander from these trails; ants rarely wander from *their* trails. Geese use specific migratory routes along which they stop at specific water habitats year after year. Families on their annual vacation use the same rest stops year after year.

The cryptic language of deoxyribonucleic acid, DNA, which codes instructions for all living cells, is no different in essence from the binary language of computers; both are encodings of information that are parsed by their respective instrumentation (i.e. Ribonucleic Acid & software respectively). DNA's nucleotides are of four chemical bases—adenine, cytosine, guanine, and thymine—and use specific pairs of these to instruct every cell in every organism to produce proteins to carry out life functions. Binary computer language is, similarly, nothing but a series of 0's and 1's that code for anything that the computer programmers desire.

The Mako shark, one of the fastest water-inhabiting organisms on the planet, has a torpedo-like shape. It is only referred to as "torpedo-like" because people, when testing their own creations, found that this general shape yielded a well-suited design for fast water-based movement. So nature, through many years of testing by means of evolution, produced a design much

140

like humans created, because both were created, through trial and error, to solve the same problem.

When the story of Daedalus and Icarus was written, how did the author decide that wings were a reasonable means of having the characters fly? When Leonardo Da Vinci was sketching the world's first schematic for a flying machine, how did he get the inspiration to develop it using wings? And as we mentioned before, a certain class of flying objects will require a specific design in order to maximize its performance relative to its particular characteristics, whether we are speaking of the B-52 and the albatross or the F-14 and the Falcon.

Branches on trees, branches of veins in the human body, branches of a river when it nears its delta—all have the same basic, characteristic design. Is this design inherently the most effective and economical within each overall system? Are there basic underlying principles within the System causing all of these "transportation" systems to assume similar forms?

Cycles involving revolutions around something, such as an electron revolving around the nucleus of an atom or the Earth revolving around the Sun, follow the same design, only in different ways.

All or Nothing

Another principle that allows systems to work effectively, and which many systems make use of, is the all-or-nothing response. Once an action is committed to, the best results come when there is a complete effort with regard to the action concerned. Imagine a person who is about to take a test, who besides thinking of the subject matter of the test, is also thinking about a relationship that just ended. Extraneous preoccupations prevent our full attention from being directed to the task at hand, with the result that neither the extraneous distraction nor the task at hand is dealt with in a manner that can produce the desired results.

Neurons fire when a certain polarity is reached within a cell, enabling neurotransmitters to be released so that there is

141

communication with the surrounding neurons. The neuron will never fire, however, unless the polarity reaches a certain point; it will not fire partially if it reaches a polarity close but not equal to the needed polarity. It either fires completely or not at all.

The Vietnam War is a good example of how people failed to take this all-or-nothing approach. The loss of the Vietnam War is largely attributed to there being a less than full commitment on the part of the United States military. The reason for this lack of full commitment was, in large part, internal conflict within the U.S. concerning the war. Because of that general lack of support for the war, the war effort was half-hearted. The same may be and indeed has been said for the current Iraq war.

When a woman becomes pregnant she does not become partially pregnant; she becomes fully pregnant. When a liquid reaches its boiling point, all of the liquid's molecules will eventually evaporate into vapor molecules if the temperature remains at boiling. When water reaches 32° Fahrenheit it completely turns to ice.

A limb, such as an arm, is constructed of a duality of muscles, in which one set contracts while the other set relaxes and vice versa. The protracting muscle extends the limb, while the contracting one brings it closer to itself. Now imagine that both muscles are in use at the same time. The forces enacted by one would interfere with the forces of the other. The muscles' purpose, which is movement, would be nullified on account of the two opposing forces fighting one another, and possibly even tearing each other apart. It is for this reason that when one throws a punch in boxing or swings a golf club, the muscles used are supposed to remain relaxed if one is to get the most out of them. A punch thrown with a mixture of triceps and biceps will result in a weaker, slower punch than one thrown with no use of the biceps. In order for the triceps to be utilized in a punch, the biceps must remain relaxed.

In other movements, however, both sets of muscles are used, existing in a balance such as in lifting up a coffee mug to ones lips or signing your signature. In these movements a balance is kept so that a stable movement can be achieved so that the coffee isn't spilt and the signature appears as it should.

Balance

A system that does not exist in a relative state of balance is a system that can be drastically altered. Ecosystems, economic markets, politics, atoms, the solar system, the universe—all exist in some form of balance, for if they did not, they likely would undergo some major event acting as a catalyst to stabilize them.

The level flight of a bird or plane is dependent on a balance between the gravity weighing down on their masses and the lift generated by their wings. A solution composed of H_2O and NaCl—that is, common table salt—exists at equilibrium in a state in which no NaCl molecules are visible because they are all equally distributed among the H_2O molecules held in place by intermolecular forces. When there are more NaCl molecules than the H_2O can integrate into its solution, NaCl molecules remain in their solid state and fall to the bottom. NaCl reached saturation levels.

Imagine bodies of water if there was a great excess of NaCl, as in the "Dead Sea," where salt washes up upon the shores of its beaches. Not as much life would exist in the oceans in that event, since most organisms' cells would tend to shrink, with most of the water inside them leaving the cell for the salty environment to attempt to achieve balance. Some life that had adapted to such an environment would exist, but not as many species would be able to handle such an extreme environment.

Imagine a party where there is not an equal balance of males and females. This system is not in balance, and is therefore likely to be much more unstable than a party composed entirely of couples. If there are ten males and four females, the natural instinct of animals, which is to find a mate, would cause rivalries to arise, as they do among other animals. Likewise, a system composed of all guys or all girls is likely to be more stable, because there would be no immediate competition for mates.

Power is a perfect study of balance. The first law of thermodynamics illustrates the balance well:

The change in internal energy of a system is equal to the heat added to the system minus the work done by the system.

This law is a direct application of the principle of *conservation of energy (or power)*. Power is neither created nor destroyed—only transferred from one entity to another.

In human society there is only a finite amount of resources, which an increasing population of now over six billion people are forced to share. The nations that have the most resource-laden lands are also the most powerful, for they control more of what others want.

In the case of individuals, however, what happens when someone with a large amount of power dies? Their money is redistributed according to their will. Sometimes this money will be given to charities, thus distributing the money (i.e., power) more widely. Other times it will remain concentrated, as in the Forbes or Bush families, being handed down generation to generation.

But power does not always come in the form of money; an individual who was a leader, for example, may have possessed some charismatic characteristic that in itself was a source of power. When they die that power is destroyed, as it cannot be handed down to subsequent generations unless it is taught. However, this power really is only in abeyance. For people always need charismatic individuals to admire and follow. The void created by this individual's death will create a vacuum, an opening, in the realm of power that will seek to be filled, usually at first by a number of individuals. Gradually, however, the strongest of these will survive and displace the others vying for the spot.

It is much like the struggle of newly born trees in a rain forest. When an older tree collapses after dying, leaving a sunny opening in the forest canopy, only one of the seedlings will be

144

able to attain sun and survive. In many ways, the sun is the most valuable resource for the growing trees in that if the sun's light is blocked before they are able to stretch their limbs above the canopy, they will die. It is usually the first ones to enter the space that succeed, much like fledgling companies in brand-new industries though many exceptions in the business world do exist.

Fish have a power hierarchy. After I acquired my first fish tank, there was a yellow African cichlid that was the terror of the fish community. All of the other fish in the 60-gallon tank were plastered against both sides of the tank, hiding among the plants and rocks, while the yellow fish would float, showing off all of his fins in a power display, right in the direct center of the tank. If any fish entered his domain, he would immediately propel himself to the fish, nipping their fins.

Another fish of the same size and species in the tank, a blue African cichlid, was much less powerful. The blue fish therefore would seek protection next to the tank's largest fish, a parrot cichlid, which was possibly eight times as large as any of the other fish, the yellow one included. Even though the parrot cichlid had powerful jaws along with a huge, though somewhat awkward body, he did not have the fighting spirit that the yellow one had. The two fish would often have bouts that would almost always end in a stalemate. In these matches the parrot cichlid was always the one on the defensive—with the blue one hiding behind him, using him as a bodyguard.

Eventually, the yellow fish became far too disruptive for the tank and was removed, being given back to the fish store. where he could eventually terrorize all of *those* fish. However, once the yellow fish, who was positioned at the extremely aggressive end of the spectrum, was gone, the blue fish, who up until this point had done nothing but run from the yellow fish, hiding behind the parrot cichlid, now stepped up in the tank's hierarchy and began his own patrols of the tank, harassing the other fish (except the parrot cichlid). His patrols of the tank were a far cry from the yellow fish's patrols, but the fact is that he never made any patrols until the yellow fish was no longer there.

The true ruler of the tank, however, was now the parrot

cichlid, as he would every now and then make a half-hearted attempt to display his power by chasing some of the other fish. His hold over the tank was strong, but he acted as a benevolent ruler. He exercised his power only to the extent of almost ceremonially displaying it within the tank community. His more lackadaisical reign, however, allowed the blue fish to also establish some degree of power within the tank, balancing the power distribution and making the power hierarchy in the tank into a more stable system. This new system existed in a somewhat multipolar state vis-à-vis the hegemony, or complete dominance, established by the yellow fish.

Individual people in a social context exercise the same sort of balancing act with respect to hierarchical power. Ever notice the person granted by many people in the room with "top dog" status? Many will circle around this person with no air of contention toward them at all. Once that person is gone, however, the people who gathered around him often take their association with the "top dog" as a means to rise in power once the "top dog" is no longer present within the group. The same is true of chicken groups with their "pecking order".

In martial arts, the two fighters exist within a system. When both are in the "on-guard" position, a slightly wavering balance exists, as each sizes the other up trying to assess the other's strengths and weaknesses. When one strikes, his system, existing as their body, goes into an unbalanced state as a limb, be it an arm or a leg, is thrown away from the body. As with any system that goes into a sudden state of imbalance, there exists the possibility that this system could be significantly altered. If the attacker's punch misses, he is left exposed to the extent that the punch was strong, giving the other fighter a moment of power when he can use the opening to inflict damage upon the attacker and thereby exercise the power that the original attacker had lost by leaving the neutral on-guard position.

The overall system consisting of both fighters is therefore in a constant state of flux, with each fighter acquiring or losing power with each move they make. If an attack is blocked, the system may return to a precarious equilibrium if the defender hesitates to respond with his own attack. The goal of both fighters is to adapt sufficiently to the other element within the system—that is, the other fighter—so as to dominate it.

A "perfect" conversation exists as a balance between listening and talking. Conversations that are not balanced tend to leave at least one party feeling uneasy or frustrated, depending on the two individuals' personalities. If one party talks endlessly, while the other party does not have a chance to express themselves, the talking party may feel fulfilled through the interaction, having expressed themselves, while the silent party feels frustrated.

Freud argued that one of the basic human desires is to feel important. If one is unable to express himself, whether in social interaction or through writing, art, music, or dance or by some other means, then that individual will exist with much pent-up emotion and will feel alienated from the world.

So in the case of a conversation wherein one party is unable to speak, the system existing as the social interaction between those two individuals may not come into existence again. The conversation is more likely to end, with the frustrated party leaving early, and the system will break apart shortly after its formation. A balanced conversation will usually last longer and is more likely to be repeated, for both parties involved will have had a chance to fulfill their need for self-expression and consequently achieve some sense of self-validation. The same is true for almost every social relationship in which both individuals in the system are on the same hierarchical level.

Z, Omega, Death, Fin, End

This book's intention is not the transfer of knowledge, but rather the conveyance of a way or perspective through which to organize one's thoughts about the world in order to understand its foundations. As soon as knowledge is fixed into a concrete form, it decays and may be broken once new knowledge surpasses the old as society advances.

Knowledge, at least human knowledge, is not a fixed

147

entity. $2 + 2$ may equal 4, at least for non-post-modernists, but will the political system be the same tomorrow as it was today? Is our knowledge of the atom the same as it was 50 years ago? Is there anyone who still thinks that we live in a geocentric universe?

The healthy mind, therefore—one that is able to understand the world—is one that remains open by adapting to changes within the System as well as in one's own knowledge. Anything that is fixed or strong without yielding is apt to break, crumble, and fall. Only the supple limb can avoid fracture; the tensed one breaks.

> *Sow an action and you reap a habit;*
> *Sow a habit and you reap a character;*
> *Sow a character and you reap a destiny.*
> *- William James*

Knowledge is the pursuit of excellence through truth—but excellence is a habit. As Vince Lombardi said, "winning is not a sometime thing, it's an all the time thing." So if one wants to know everything—or achieve anything else, for that matter—the desire to do so must become part of the person; it must be visible in the eyes as a fire burning inside. Reading or enrolling in a class are good ways to learn, but a continuous dedication instead of some fleeting activity is better.

As a final thought—as a final means of merging one's consciousness with the world—consider that the person that you were, are, and will be has in no way anything to do with you. We are products of the System—of our environments—existing as extraordinarily intricately built stimulus-response machines that act, think, and are because of everyone and everything else. For the person that you are, existing as your body and consciousness was created by every single entity that you have ever been in contact with, directly or indirectly.

This is a difficult concept for human beings to accept, because the notion of free will is so ingrained into society's belief system. Additionally, no one wants to believe that the only things that we all think we have control over, our thoughts, beliefs, and actions, are things that we actually have *no* control over. It is a disillusioning thought and admittingly one with much scrutiny.

Each one of us was created from the sperm and egg of two individuals that were not us. Subsequently, we grew up within a certain environment that skewed our personality and beliefs in a certain direction. Imagine if a Christian who was born in the United States came back as someone who had now been born in the Middle East. The beliefs that the U.S. native would have if (s)he had instead been born in the Middle East would be completely different and statistics tell us that they most likely would be Muslim. Every action that one takes, including actions that the individual considers spontaneous, was conceived by something other than one's Self.

Free will does not exist. It is only something people cling to as their own, in a world where no one really has anything. The realization that you and everyone else are automatons functioning as part of an extremely intricate System of stimulus and response, with your own genetic code as a baseline, is exceptionally important for one's ability to understand everything. Viewing yourself in the third person allows information about yourself to enter your consciousness as you observe without acting. The dissolution of the Self is the final step to obtaining an understanding of everything. Without the Self, your desires, fears, elations, and pains fade, leaving an unbiased perspective of the world.

We are all the same, floating along in this ever-changing yet never-changing System. Our only means of connection with the outside world is a four-pound mass that we have labeled a brain. We exist as, and we are, our consciousness, an electrical storm *within* the brain, producing a multi-sensory reality for us to experience as outsiders trapped by our own limitations within a body. To understand everything in the vastness of this world we need to understand the building blocks, because these are the entities through which everything exists and operates.

This is the understanding of everything.

Notes on Sources

A View to Everything...

- "A Way is a guide..." Lao Tzu, *Tao te Ching.* ca. 400 B.C.
- "At any moment..." Ashby, F.G. (2003). *Cognitive Neuroscience.* Retrieved from the University of California at Santa Barbara.
- "oral fixation..." Sigmund Freud, Psychosexual Stage Theory. *Three Essays on Sexuality*: 1915.
- "The adept understands ten..." Yamamoto Tsunetomo, *Hagakure.* 1719.

The Mind & Self...

- "Oneself... the foundation..." Douglas MacArthur
- "Self as Known/Knower..." William James, *Principles of Psychology.* 1890.
- "Estrogen..." U.S. Dept. of Health & Human Services (womenshealth.gov), *Menstruation and the Menstrual Cycle.* 2002
- "Testosterone..." Dr. John M. Berardi, Ph.D., *The Big T, Pt. II: How your Lifestyle influences your Testosterone Levels.* 2000.
- "Reptile breeding..." Philippe de Vosjoli, *The General Care and Maintenance of Ball Pythons.* Advanced Vivarium Systems, 1990
- "default sex is female..." Allgeier/Allgeier, *Sexual Interactions, 2nd Ed.* Chapter 5, pg. 125. DC Heath & Co., 1988.
- "Soy & Estrogen..." Aldercreutz H., Gorbach S. L., Goldin B. R., Woods M. N., Dwyer J. T., Hämäläinen E. *Estrogen metabolism and excretion in oriental and Caucasian women.* J. Natl. Cancer Inst., *86:* 1076-1082, 1994.
- "Testosterone & alcohol..." Dr. John M. Berardi, Ph.D., *The Big T, Pt. II: How your Lifestyle influences your Testosterone Levels.* 2000.
- "drug dependency..." Di Chiara G., Dopamine in disturbances of food and drug motivated behavior: a case of homology? *Physiol Behav.* 2005 Sep 15; 86(1-2): 9-10.
- "age factors in dopamine..." Hemby, Scott E., Trojanowski, John Q., & Ginsberg, Stephen D. Neuron-Specific Age-

Related Decreases in Dopamine Receptor Subtype mRNAs. *The Journal of Comparative Neurology 456*:176-183 (2003).

- "Conditioned response..." Ivan Pavlov, *Work of the Digestive Glands.* 1897.
- "night/day melatonin cycle..." Delagrange, P., & B. Guardiola-Lemaitre. Melatonin, Its Receptors, and Relationships with Biological Rhythm Disorders. *Clinical Neuropharmacology* 20(December 1997): 482-510.
- "SAD..." Rosenthal NE, Sack DA, et al.: Seasonal Affective Disorder: A Description of the Syndrome and Preliminary Findings with Light Therapy. Arch Gen Psychiatry 1984; 41:72--80.
- "business lighting..." Jeff Meer. The light touch; lighting affects your work, the way you deal with others, how comfortable you are and even your mental and physical health. *Psychology Today* (September 1985).
- "amnesics sense of self..." Klein, S. B., Loftus, J., & Kihlstrom, J.F.. Self-knowledge of an amnesic patient: Toward a neuropsychology of personality and social psychology. *Journal of Experimental Psychology: General,* 1996 125(3), 250-260.
- "Self...lord of chariot..." *The Seven Military Classics of Ancient China.* Westview Press, 1993.
- "Irregular heartbeat..." Simone de Beauvoir, *The Second Sex.* 1949.
- "You love your spouse..." Various Writers, *The Upanishads.* ca. 1000 B.C.
- "what is color..." Alex Byrne & David R. Hilbert (editors), *Readings on Color: The Science of Color* (volume 2), MIT Press, 1997.
- "rods & cones..." Hecht, Eugene. *Optics*, 2nd Ed, Addison Wesley, 1987.
- "I think therefore I am." René Descartes, *Discourse on Method.* 1637.
- "Peel away layers..." Mohandas K. Gandhi, *The Bhagavad Gita According to Gandhi.* Berkeley Hills Books. 2000.

Divisions & Classifications...
- "Time has no divisions..." Thomas Mann.
- See #8.

- "Schizophrenia/creativity..." Chadwick, P.K. *Schizophrenia: A Positive Perspective.* London: Routledge (1997).
- "drugs increase dopamine..." Di Chiara G., Dopamine in disturbances of food and drug motivated behavior: a case of homology? *Physiol Behav.* 2005 Sep 15; 86(1-2): 9-10.
- "first single-celled orgs..." Biological development. Encyclopædia Britannica. 2006. Encyclopædia Britannica Premium Service. 24 Jan. 2006 <http://www.britannica.com/eb/article?tocId=63710>.
- "Egyptian embalming..." Iskander, Zaky *An X-Ray Atlas of the Royal Mummies"* Univ of Chicago (1980).
- "Chaos & Taoism..." James Gleik, *Chaos.* Penguin Books. 1987.
- "Greeks fascination w/..." Morris Kline, *Mathematics for the Nonmathematician.* Dover Publications Inc. 1967.
- "Da Vinci..." Richter, Irma A.. *The Notebooks of Leonardo Da Vinci.* Oxford Univ. Press. 1952.
- "Descartes..." Chávez-Arvizo, Enrique. *Descartes: Key Philosophical Writings.* Wordsworth Classics. 1997.
- "Adam Smith..." Smith, Adam. *An Inquiry into the Nature and Causes of The Wealth of Nations.* Univ. of Chicago Press. 1976.
- "Taoist philosophy..." Cleary, Thomas. *The Essential Tao.* Harper Collins. 1993.
- "Love, the merging of..." Sigmund Freud, *Civilization & its Discontents.* 1930.
- "Moses ascends Mt. Sinai..." Various writers, *The Bible.* ca. 500 B.C. – 250 A.D.

Systems...
- "Who sees with equal..." Alexander Pope, *Essay on Man.* 1734.
- "Systems..." Michael Gerber, *The E-Myth Revisited.* Harper Collins. 2001.
- "Supply & demand..." Adam Smith, *The Wealth of Nations.* 1776.
- "Da Vinci..." Richter, Irma A.. *The Notebooks of Leonardo Da Vinci.* Oxford Univ. Press. 1952.
- "electron tube." Encyclopædia Britannica. 2006.

Encyclopædia Britannica Premium Service. 25 Jan. 2006 http://www.britannica.com/eb/article?tocId=9106024.
* "Simplicity resides within…" James Gleik, *Chaos*. Penguin Books. 1987.

Duality…
* "Knowledge has two extremes." Blaise Pascal.
* "What is good?" Aristotle, *Nicomachean Ethics*. ca. 350 B.C.
* "Earth, wind, fire, water…" Wikipedia. *Classical Element*. 2006. http://en.wikipedia.org/wiki/Classical_elements
* "self-validation…" Robert B. Cialdini, *Influence: Science & Practice*. pgs 150-152. Allyn & Bacon. 2001.
* "electrons/outer shell…" Pauling, Linus. *General Chemistry*. Dover. 1970.
* "Joking…" Sigmund Freud, *Jokes & Their Relation to the Unconscious*. 1905.

Cycles…
* "All things have their…" François Rabelais.
* "To everything, there is a season…" Various writers, *The Bible*. ca. 500 B.C. – 250 A.D.
* "Laws of motion…" Isaac Newton, *The Principia*. 1687.
* "Golden Rule…" Various writers, *The Bible*. ca. 500 B.C. – 250 A.D.
* "Four chief virtues…" Marcus Aurelius, *Meditations*. 180.
* "As soon as we posit ourselves…" Jean-Paul Satre, *Being & Nothingness*. Washington Square Press. 1943.
* See #8.
* See #26.

Who, What, Why, Where, & How…
* "The best friends I…" Ralph Waldo Emerson.
* "If I feel I can…" René Descartes, *On the Direction of the Mind*. 1628.
* "Perfect practice makes…" John Wooden, *Wooden: A Lifetime of Observations and Reflections on and off the Court*. Contemporary Books. 1997.
* "Desire… ultimate evil…" Sayings of Buddha,

Dhammapada. ca. 252 B.C.
- "Influence principles..." Robert B. Cialdini, *Influence: Science & Practice.* Allyn & Bacon. 2001.
- "A goose is still a goose..." Henry David Thoreau, *Walden.* 1854.
- "Tree-hoppers..." The Audubon Society, *Field Guide to North American Insects & Spiders.* Alfred A. Knopf. 1980.
- "Sherlock Holmes..." Sir Arthur Conan Doyle, *Sherlock Holmes.* 1891-1927.
- "The consciousness is ever..." Jean-Paul Satre, *Being & Nothingness.* Washington Square Press. 1943.

The Parts Become the Whole...
- "In the unitive state..." Various Writers, *The Upanishads.* ca. 1000 B.C.
- "Do I..." Whitman, Walt. *Song of Myself.* 1855.
- "Butterfly effect..." James Gleik, *Chaos.* Penguin Books. 1987.
- "Animals & computers..." Norbert Wiener, *Cybernetics: or Control and Communication in the Animal and the Machine.* The MIT Press. 1948.
- "action potential..." Matthews, Gary G. *Neurobiology: Molecules, Cells, & Systems* 2nd ed. Blackwell Publishers. 2001.
- "Sow an action..." William James, *Principles of Psychology.* 1890.
- "Winning is not..." Lombardi, Vince. *What it takes to be Number One.* 1970.
- "Free will does not exist..." B.F. Skinner, *Beyond Freedom & Dignity.* Bantom Books. 1971.

Other books to read:

- *The E-Myth Revisited*, by Michael Gerber
- *Chaos*, by James Gleik
- *Tao te Ching*, by Thomas Cleary
- *Influence*, by Robert Cialdini
- *Origin of Species*, by Charles Darwin
- *Meditations*, by Marcus Aurelius
- *On the Method of Discourse*, by Descartes
- *The Ego and Id*, by Sigmund Freud
- *Beyond Freedom and Dignity*, by BF Skinner
- *Nicomachean Ethics*, by Aristotle
- *Dhammapada,* by Buddha
- *The Wealth of Nations,* by Adam Smith
- *Thus Spake Zarathustra, by Friedrich Nietzsche*

Future A Brief Guide™ books:

A Brief Guide to POWER

Power dominates and controls the world. Every action or event is a result of some sort of power being exercised. Whether the power exacted is in the brain in the form of electrical impulses across neurons, the constant pulling power of gravity upon Earth or the military and economic might of a country. All of these powers are related and follow similar principles.

A Brief Guide to Life

Ask what life is and you'll receive a multitude of answers. Life is an electro-chemical occurrence, our consciousness, our genetic makeup, our experiences, and a miracle. Life can also be exhilarating, boring, joyful, fragile, sorrowful, and terrifying. There are few definites in life and that's what makes it all of these things at one point or another and sometimes all at once. We all have been given the gift of life for the price of that life.

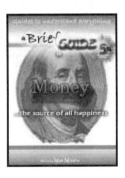

A Brief Guide to Money

For some, money is an all consuming matter and for good reason. Money determines the survival of every human being. Money buys us everything from food to shelter and everything in between. It unlocks doors unavailable to those without money. Money may not buy happiness, but it buys comfort and expanded possibilities.

A Brief Guide to Understand Everything
Order Form

Fax Orders: (310) 826-0698 (send this form)
Email Orders: orders@abriefguide.com
Postal Orders:

> A Brief Guide Publishing
> ATTN: Order Processing
> PO Box 765
> Los Angeles, CA 90049, USA

Please send me: 1 __ 2 __ 3 __ other _____, copies of A Brief Guide to Understand Everything. Per copy price $12.95 (excluding tax)

Sales tax: Please add 8.25% for products shipped to California addresses. (Tax total per copy = $1.00).

SHIPPING - $3.99 will be charged for all continental US addresses. Int'l rates will vary.

My order total, including shipping, is $_____.

I understand that my payment will not be processed until the date the book is shipped.

Name: _____

Address: _____

City: _____ State: _____ Zip: _____

Telephone: _____

Email: _____

Please send more information concerning when they become available:
___: ABG documentaries
___: ABG books
___: MAHA books

Payment: ____ Cheque _____ Money Order _____Credit Card:
____ Visa ____ Mastercard ____ AMEX ____ Discover

Card number: _____

Name on Card:_____ Exp. Date: _____

www.understandeverything.com